Expert Systems
A Practical Introduction

Peter S. Sell

MACMILLAN

First published 1985
Reprinted 1986

Published by
Higher and Further Education Division
MACMILLAN PUBLISHERS LTD
Houndmills, Basingstoke, Hampshire RG21 2XS
and London
Companies and representatives
throughout the world

Printed in Hong Kong

British Library Cataloguing in Publication Data
Sell, Peter S.
Expert systems: a practical introduction.
1. Expert systems (Computer science)
I. Title
001.64   QA76.9.E96
ISBN 0–333–37264–6

Contents

Preface

Expert systems represent a new opportunity in computing. They open up avenues of application so far closed and allow new problems to be tackled. Although the ideas underpinning the technique are still in ferment, the techniques they employ have been in use for two decades or more. Nevertheless, it was only recently that they achieved prominence in the public eye and started to be exploited by commerce and industry. One result of their neglect is that practical information on the subject is hard to come by and, as is often the case with a little-known territory, the subject appears more mysterious and forbidding than its nature warrants. It is true that, in the large area that expert systems span, complex and powerful techniques can be found at work. Nevertheless, the theme of this book is that in at least one mode of use, namely that of the so called 'single shot' advisory systems, the appropriate techniques used to give form to such systems lie close to the mainstream of software engineering. What is undoubtedly difficult and new is how to give them content, how to imbue them with knowledge. The situation will remain thus until generally applicable methods of knowledge acquisition are found.

This book is aimed at the advanced undergraduate or new practitioner. I have assumed that he (by which term I mean here and all through the book 'he or she') is a competent programmer who is familiar with the software development life cycle, at home with basic data structures, and conversant enough with high-level languages not to baulk at notation that is eclectic but whose meaning, I hope, is self-evident. I also assume that he has at least a nodding acquaintance with compilers and what they can do. The book is meant to give the reader sufficient insight and practical guidance to enable him to construct an expert system shell using his favourite programming language. To allow the latter, I have refrained from using some powerful facilities - such as 'eval' - which could simplify the algorithms but could create problems in implementation if not provided by the host language.

The first three chapters introduce the topic through an overview of Artificial Intelligence, a brief history and characterisation of expert systems. Chapter 4 addresses the question of how to develop and maintain these systems. Chapters 5 and 7 tackle the technical issues. They concentrate on problems unique to the field and touch lightly on matters that the reader may already be familiar with or can obtain information on from other, specialist sources. The last chapter gives some help with assessing new applications. In my experience, there is never a shortage of ideas for using expert systems, so what is needed is not a catalogue of possibilities but advice on how to assess them. There are a few questions to test the reader's understanding and, where there is material for further reading, I give references after each chapter. An aggregate list of these is given at the end of the book. I have limited references to those available to the general public.

I am, of course, responsible for the words and ideas but, like any author, I owe indebtedness to many others - too many to name them all. I would like to express my appreciation to members of the Knowledge Engineering Group of SPL for their help, to my superiors and colleagues for their encouragement, to SPL-Insight for acting as a sounding board, but most of all to my wife, Frances, for correcting my more egregious errors and for continuing to treat with love and patience her husband turned lodger.

Finally, because so much is still in the melting pot, this book can hope to be no more than a snapshot of what we know today. I hope, nevertheless, that it will help those who wish to get their feet wet, and provide for others at least a clearly focused target for refutation and growth.

Southmoor, 1984.   Peter S. Sell

1 Origins

1.1 Artificial Intelligence

People have always been fascinated by the prospect of intelligent artefacts. Wolfgang von Kempelen's chess playing automaton for many years astonished and puzzled 18th century Europe. It was later proved a fraud: it concealed, with the aid of ingenious mechanical contrivances, a human player. In those days the technology did not exist to make an intelligent machine. Even at the beginning of this century, when Karel Capek wrote about his robot - and gave us the term to use - an intelligent machine was still considered to be a pipe-dream. But with the arrival of computers during the second World War, man-made intelligence became, for the first time, plausible. In 1950 Alan Turing published his paper *Can a Machine Think?* showing by this action that it was a legitimate subject, at least for philosophical speculation. But where his interest was that of a mathematician and logician, computer scientists' interest was much more practical. Seeing how readily computers could be used to solve problems that were too tedious for humans, speculation began as to whether they could also be used to solve problems that humans found too difficult. Speculation gave way to experiments, and after another six years the first artificial intelligence programs appeared. The initial successes opened the floodgates: within a few years we had programs playing chess, checkers, proving theorems of logic and geometry, solving integrals, learning concepts - performing tasks that up till then could only be done by man. Artificial Intelligence (AI) was born.

Some hailed it as the greatest advance man has ever seen and looked forward to the day - in the not-too-distant future - when computers would help the thinker in the same way as machines help the labourer. They looked forward to computers tackling intellectual tasks that only a genius could handle, solving problems that baffled the brightest and the best. And with some justification: the early signs were most encouraging.

The first significant achievement came with GPS (General Problem Solver), a program created by Newell, Shaw and Simon in 1957. Their program could solve puzzles and brainteasers - like Missionaries and Cannibals, or Towers of Hanoi - and tackle significant problems - like proving theorems in predicate calculus. GPS, as its name implies, was created to serve as a general, by which they meant a domain-independent problem solver. Although successful in some areas, there were many problems that it could not solve. GPS sought its power from general problem-solving techniques, like means-end analysis. The generally held opinion was that to increase its power all we needed to do was to add more methods to its armoury.

This turned out to be wrong because it was based on two mistaken assumptions: that we know what other methods to add and that the general methods we know of are powerful enough to solve many different problems. The first mistaken assumption was uncovered very quickly. The methods used by GPS were imitative of the methods people use to solve problems. To endow it with more power, other general methods were needed that similarly mimic human thought. But to imitate any mechanism, we have to know how it works. Now, although we solve problems every day, we are not fully aware of the methods we use. Therefore, to achieve their first aim, to create an intelligent artefact, AI researchers had to add a second item to their agenda: to find out how the human mind works. These two aims still stand today: to create intelligent artefacts and to create models of the human mind.

To uncover the second assumption took nearly ten years. In 1964 Joshua Lederberg, Professor of Genetics at Stanford University, devised a program to enumerate all possible, but legal, configurations of a given set of atoms. He called his program DENDRAL, short for DENDRitic ALgorithm. It was designed to provide chemists with a checklist for the compounds that they were trying to identify. A year later the project's terms of reference were dramatically broadened. Its goal was now to tackle the real problem: how to identify molecular compounds from analytical data. And its methods were now to include Artificial Intelligence techniques. The work proceeded well and DENDRAL became a powerful intellectual aid that could solve tough problems in a dark corner of science which had not yet been illuminated by a verified theory.

Scientific revolutions have a habit of sneaking in through the back door. Probably no-one on the DENDRAL project realised that AI had arrived at a watershed. That realisation came later. Looking at it with the benefit of hindsight, we can see clearly the tremendous contribution that this project made: it succeeded largely because it sought solutions in the opposite direction to everyone else. When others sought general, *domain-independent* methods for solving problems, it sought specific, *domain-dependent* methods. Some years later Professor Feigenbaum christened this change of direction the 'paradigm shift in AI', the paradigm shift from power-based techniques to knowledge-based ones. The new direction was successful, and it laid the foundations for expert systems.

The change of tack paid off: by the late 1960s DENDRAL was creating successful hypotheses on the molecular structure of unknown compounds from their mass spectrograms. The next decade saw the development of MYCIN and PROSPECTOR, two systems that many consider to be the intellectual models for expert systems. But before we look at these systems in more detail, let us consider why this paradigm shift was necessary.

1.2 Problem solving

Our interest in models of human cognition and in intelligent artefacts serves one utilitarian purpose: to solve problems. We hope that what we can learn from these two will enable us to solve problems better, to solve problems that we could not solve before, and to build programs or machines to solve them for us. But how do we, or programs, go about solving problems? If we are interested in building such programs, we ought to spend some time on this question.

Turing's paper addressed the question only indirectly: can a machine think? Nevertheless, he gave impetus to an inquiry that turned out to be not only interesting but also fruitful, for it encouraged closer scrutiny of closely related ideas: thought, intelligence, and mental activities of all kinds. On the other hand, the effort put into increasing the power of GPS began to organise our ideas about problem solving, and identified several generic methods that we employ. Thus began a process of exploration that still continues today. But even the little way that we have travelled gives us a better view of this fascinating subject.

We now know that we employ several distinct methods of solving problems. The simplest method we could call the *algorithmic method*. We use this method daily. We all possess ready-made algorithms for solving problems like tying shoe-laces, multiplying numbers, booking a holiday, making a telephone call, solving simultaneous equations, driving a car, and so on. Some of our algorithms are very simple, some highly complex, but they are all composed of sequences of actions - with possible decision and branching points - which we had to learn or discover. Leaving aside algorithms requiring physical actions - which fall in the realm of robotics - these methods can be readily implemented on computers.

To some degree, these problems are rather mundane. Interesting problems often do not have algorithmic solutions; nevertheless, they must be solved. How do we set about solving these? When we have no ready made solution, we resort to exploration by trial-and-error. Depending on how systematic we are in its use, the method can range from the desultory to the rigorous. It can engage us in a few random stabs at the solution, and it can methodically lead us to examine all possible cases. Its more rigorous form is known as the *generate-and-test method*. The idea behind this is very simple: we generate candidate solutions to the problem and test each candidate for acceptability. The method is powerful in that if a solution exists, we are guaranteed to find it. But it suffers from the danger of *combinatorial explosion*: there may be more cases to generate and test than we have resources for. It may be possible to produce the collected works of Shakespeare by the labours of a troop of monkeys, but it is likely to take longer than we care to wait. The simplest game-playing programs employ this method: they generate all possible moves, all possible replies to those moves, and so on, until all moves terminate in a win, loss, or draw; then a path can be selected which is sure to lead to a win or to avoid a loss. For simple games, like noughts and crosses, the method is practicable; for others, computers tend to run out of space, time, or both.

For practical purposes we need to constrain the number of cases that we generate and test. The constraint can vary. One method uses evaluation criteria that allow us to ignore subsets of the candidates. This form of constraint is often used in game-playing programs to prune the tree of possibilities. Whereas this method avoids generating candidates, another method uses similar evaluation criteria to bias the generation of new candidates. This is the method used in hill-climbing algorithms where each new candidate, if it is to merit consideration, has to better the last one. This, too, reduces the number of generated candidates. These are only two examples of many possibilities, but they all share a common aim: to bring the variety of the solution space within the capabilities of the machine.

The most interesting variant for us is a third method in which the constraint comes from knowledge of the situation. This is the way that expert systems prevent combinatorial explosion: DENDRAL uses the laws of chemistry to eliminate impossible bondings of elements; MYCIN uses the diagnostic rules of medicine to eliminate impossible symptom-disease combinations. We make use of this method more readily and more frequently than we use pruning or hill-climbing. For example, when planning a trip from London to Bristol, we dispense with all routes leading north, east, or south by simply noting that Bristol lies to the west. Then we use our knowledge of traffic patterns to eliminate minor routes. By this and similar stratagems we can arrive at an acceptable route from a huge number of possibilities.

GPS uses the generate-and-test method. It also uses some methods of constraint. For instance, it will not try to apply an operator, such as transferring two cannibals across the river, if the conditions are not right for such an application, such as there are no cannibals to transfer. But its rules of constraint, because it is a general-purpose program, have to be generally applicable, and that means weak. The constraints used in DENDRAL, MYCIN, and other expert systems are powerful precisely because they are specific to the domain.

Interesting and difficult problems have large solution spaces. If we wish to tackle these spaces methodically we need to employ some form of constraint. As generally applicable constraints tend to be weak, we have to resort to those dictated by the domain. Thus we can see why the paradigm shift from domain-independent to domain-dependent methods was necessary. The efficacy of expert systems shows that it was also successful.

Question

Some describe Artificial Intelligence as a branch of psychology: computational cognition. Does this view tally with the aims stated in this chapter?

Further reading

Turing's paper, describing what we now know as the "Turing test" was first published in *Mind* (October, 1950); it and many other interesting papers are reproduced in Edward A. Feigenbaum and Julian Feldman's collection, *Computers and Thought* (McGraw-Hill, 1963). A full description of GPS can be read in George Ernst and Allen Newell's ACM Monograph, *GPS: A Case Study in Generality and Problem Solving* (Academic Press, 1969). The DENDRAL Project is described in a book by Robert K. Lindsay, Bruce G. Buchanan, Edward A. Feigenbaum and Joshua Lederberg, *Applications of Artificial Intelligence for Organic Chemistry* (McGraw-Hill, 1980).

2   Examples

There are over fifty expert systems reported to be in
use today, and their number is rapidly increasing.
Finding examples is, consequently, not difficult. But
there are four systems that merit special attention:
they are, so to speak, the 'grand originals': DENDRAL,
MYCIN, PROSPECTOR, and R1. In this chapter we will look
at these four.

2.1 DENDRAL

We have already met DENDRAL in chapter 1.   There we saw
that work on it started in 1964 at Stanford University.
Its aim is to hypothesise on the possible molecular
structure of a compound. When confronted with an
unknown compound, the first task of a chemist is to
establish what are its constituent atoms and what are
their relative ratios.   To do this, he performs
analytical tests and experiments.   One instrument that
is often used is the mass spectrometer. Its precise
operation need not concern us here; stated very simply,
it plots the relative frequency of different atoms and
molecular fragments in the compound. From this
information, the chemist has to estimate its
constituent atoms and their arrangement in the
molecule. His task reminds one of those puzzles in
which from the combined and relative ages in a family
we need to find the ages of its members. But, of
course, it is far more complex than that. The 'family'
is large - all the known atoms - and their possible
relationships fill volumes. But the most important fact
to remember is that there is no scientific algorithm by
which we can proceed from mass spectra to molecular
structure.
     Originally, DENDRAL was designed to enumerate all
possible configurations of a set of atoms observing the

rules of chemical valence. This enumeration could then serve as a checklist of possibilities for the chemist. Strictly speaking, DENDRAL is now not one program but a family of programs. But the original algorithm is at the centre of this family. The other programs significantly extended its power. The most important extension was that which took the generated set of *possible* cases and reduced it to a set of *likely* ones. To do that, it had to store and make use of *heuristics* or rules based on chemical facts, on the laws of chemistry, and on the judgement and experience of experts.

DENDRAL is a success story. The results derived from its use are cited in over 50 scientific papers, which attests not only to its usefulness but also to its scientific credentials. It is in regular and routine use. The number of its users was expanding so rapidly that in 1983 a separate company was set up for its distribution and continued enhancement.

2.2 MYCIN

One of the most common forms of illness we suffer from is bacterial infection. Thanks to advances in medicine, we now have a large number of antimicrobial and their better-known subset of antibiotic agents ready to combat such infections. However, such a wide range presents the physician not only with greater freedom of choice but also with a greater problem of selection. If there were a single antimicrobial agent effective against all infectious bacteria, the problem of selection would not exist. Alas, there is no such wonder-drug. What is more, one drug may be highly effective against one but not other types of bacteria. The physician, therefore, has to be careful in his choice. Furthermore, effectiveness is only one of his criteria: he also has to take into account the patient's allergies, his current drug intake, and similar contra-indications. MYCIN was designed to help the physician with this problem.

If we look closely at the physician's task, we can see that he has four decisions to make: does the patient suffer from bacterial infection, what organism is responsible, which drugs may be appropriate, and which of these to administer. MYCIN was designed to assist all four decisions. The way that it assists is as follows. On the basis of patient data and test results, it arrives at a conclusion to all four questions. It displays these conclusions and its degree of certainty about them. It can then display, on request, the line of reasoning that it followed to reach those conclusions, the rules it used *en route*, the alternatives it rejected, and even appropriate references to articles and other publications that serve as warrant to those rules. Armed with this information, the physician is in an excellent position to form his own judgement.

Work started on MYCIN in 1972 at Stanford University. Its name derives from the suffix commonly occurring in the names of many antimicrobial agents (as in 'streptomycin'). The rules that it uses were obtained from specialists in the field of bacterial infection. In a series of tests, selected from cases of blood infection, MYCIN's conclusions were compared with those of specialist and non-specialist medical practitioners. MYCIN performed extremely well in these tests, at least as well as the experts and significantly better than non-specialists.

In spite of its proven track record, MYCIN is not in clinical use. The main reason for this is that physicians are not inclined to use computers for tasks that they feel they can do themselves. There are other reasons as well. It needs a large machine (the original implementation was on a PDP-10 with 256K memory); it takes 20-30 minutes per consultation; and it has no access to patients' records, so all patient data has to be entered during the consultation. Its main use is as a teaching aid: with its excellent explanation facilities it can tutor as well as represent the most up-to-date and most easy-to-use reference on the subject.

2.3 PROSPECTOR

PROSPECTOR is a computer-based consulting system designed to aid geologists in their search for ore deposits and in their evaluation of the mineral potential of large geographic areas. It was developed at the Stanford Reseach Institute from 1978 onwards. Like MYCIN, it is a conversational system based on rules obtained from specialists. PROSPECTOR is not really just one system; it accommodates several distinct geological models: three different sandstone uranium deposit models, prophyry copper, and prophyry molybdenum models have been reported on.

The task of a geologist in assessing a site is made difficult by the fact that indications for a particular deposit are rarely unambiguous, nor are all of them always present. So he has to balance favourable and contrary signs, weigh their relative importance, and come to a probability judgement. The number of factors that he has to consider are usually large and their significance relative. These factors made the acquisition of rules equally problematical and difficult. Nevertheless, when the models were submitted to tests against known sites of exploration and against the judgement of experts, PROSPECTOR was found to be in agreement within 7 per cent.

PROSPECTOR is available for consultation for a very modest fee.

2.4 R1

R1 (also known as XCON) is perhaps the most successful expert system in use. It was developed by John McDermott and his colleagues at the Carnegie-Mellon University (CMU) at the request of Digital Equipment Corporation (DEC). When DEC brought out their VAX range of computers, they centred their marketing around the concept of customer choice. They wanted to allow the customer as much freedom as possible in deciding what items of equipment should make up his particular installation. This freedom of choice created a difficult problem for DEC: customer requirements are merely an outline of what constitutes a working configuration. Customer orders, therefore, have to be translated into complete and coherent configurations. Some equipment needs to be added, like power supplies, cabinets and cables; other equipment needs to be specified in greater detail, like translating disk storage requirements into disk units and controllers; site layout needs to be worked out; cable lengths and destinations specified. In short, a lot of detail needs to be worked on, which requires knowledge of the range of equipment offered and the constraints that it has to observe.

People at DEC saw immediately that unless they mechanised this process, they would have a lot of their staff tied up doing it, and probably not very well at that. They tried using traditional methods first. But after recognising that they were getting nowhere, they called on CMU for help. The result of their cooperation is Rl: a knowledge-based VAX configuration system.

Discussions on Rl started around December 1978. It went into operation in January 1980. It had about 400 rules at that time, a number that has since grown to over 4000. DEC calculate that by 1984 they would have required 80 more staff without Rl, and they are convinced that it does the job much better than people could do it. Indeed, they are so convinced of the power of the technique that they intend to employ it up and downstream. Upstream, to help the sales force and the customer to select coherent configurations that best match requirements; downstream to help with site preparation, to schedule the production and delivery of the configurations on order, to help factory scheduling, material and stores control, and so on.

2.5 Summary

The four systems described in this chapter are important for at least two reasons: they proved that the expert system technique is useful in solving real-world problems, and they provided models of implementation for others to follow. Many of today's systems are directly based on them, not only in specific applications but also in the so-called expert system 'shells', the toolsets that ease the production of expert system applications.

Further reading

A description of DENDRAL and the history of the DENDRAL project is available in a book by Robert K. Lindsay, Bruce G. Buchanan, Edward A. Feigenbaum and Joshua Lederberg, *Applications of Artificial Intelligence for Organic Chemistry* (McGraw-Hill, 1980). On MYCIN see Edward H. Shortliffe's book, *Computer-Based Medical Consultations: MYCIN* (Elsevier, 1976). Detailed material on PROSPECTOR and Rl is not easily accessible. A good, albeit brief, article is by Richard Duda, John Gaschnig and Peter Hart, 'Model Design in the PROSPECTOR Consultant System for Mineral Exploration', in *Expert Systems in the Micro-electronic Age*, ed. Donald Michie (Edinburgh University Press, 1979). The article by John McDermott, "XSEL: a computer sales person's assistant", in *Machine Intelligence 10*, eds J.E. Hayes, Donald Michie and Y-H Pao (Ellis Horwood Ltd. and John Wiley & Sons, 1982) gives a lot of information on R1.

3 Characteristics

The purpose of this chapter is to explore the concept
of expert systems. It would be gratifying if we could
start with an exact definition and proceed from there.
However, Artificial Intelligence is such a young
discipline - mere decades rather than centuries old -
and expert systems such a recent application of this
discipline that there has not been sufficient time for
terminology to crystallise. Concepts of the field are
still shifting and boundaries are hazy; so any attempt
at strict and exact definitions is doomed to failure.

Fortunately, we do not need strict and exact
definitions, just a sufficient grasp to handle the
concepts comfortably. What we are seeking is insight,
not rigour. The purpose here is more to characterise
expert systems in enough detail to allow us to
recognise true examples and to reject false pretenders.

We shall approach our search for this appreciation
by three steps. Expert systems display essential and
desirable characteristics: essential ones, without
which they could not be called expert systems and
desirable ones without which, in most cases, they would
not be usable. Sections 3.1 and 3.2 describe these
characteristics, while section 3.3 classifies expert
systems.

3.1 Essential characteristics

Before proceeding with this task, let us first dispose
of what, to some, is a constant source of irritation:
the name *expert systems*. Like many terms in computer
science and other fields, it arose by accident rather
than design. It may not be a good term, but it is the
term that people use, and we have to accept it until
somebody comes up with a better one. To argue for or
against it is futile. So, instead of debating its

merits or otherwise, let us turn our attention to what the essential characteristics are.

As mentioned before, Artificial Intelligence has two different products: models of human cognition and intelligent artefacts. Expert systems belong to the latter. They were created not so much to model how experts set about solving problems and, hence, to understand better the workings of an expert's mind, but for the practical purpose of reaping the benefits from the expert thought embedded in a computer system. Of course, the two areas interact with beneficial side-effects. Building expert systems is in a sense creating a model of expert thought, and this allows us to cast better models of cognition. And better models of cognition, obtained perhaps from a different field, allow us to build expert systems better. But all that is, so to speak, the icing on the cake.

Intelligent artefacts are produced primarily to solve problems, and this is the main reason for building expert systems. Of the two main methods of problem solving used by intelligent artefacts, namely general or domain-independent and special or domain-specific, expert systems come into the second, domain-specific category. A large class of these domain-specific methods relies on knowledge culled from human experts; they are known as *knowledge-based systems* or even *intelligent knowledge-based systems* (abbreviated as KBS and IKBS). Expert systems form a subclass of knowledge based systems, a subclass that focuses on a single area, which restricts itself to a single domain of expertise.

If the system is not knowledge based, it should not be called an expert system. The main difficulty with this injunction is how to tell knowledge-based systems from others. Knowledge, unfortunately, is a slippery concept; philosophers have sought in vain to define it for thousands of years. In order to avoid philosophical difficulties about just what is knowledge, practitioners treat as knowledge any rules, facts, truths, reasons, and heuristics gleaned from experts that have been found useful in the domain of solving problems.

The domain in which an expert system operates is a *particular* domain. Individual expert systems are employed to diagnose blood diseases, to monitor iron-lung patients, and to advise mineral explorers; each is a well-defined and sharply differentiated area of expertise. MYCIN can say nothing about cancer,

PROSPECTOR nothing about oil, even though these topics lie close to the areas of competence of these systems.

Furthermore, expert system domains are areas of *expertise*, in contrast to common sense; expert systems typically possess very little common sense. DART I - a machine diagnostic program - will not tell you to stop testing because the equipment is on fire. Some view this as a serious shortcoming. Nevertheless, expert systems solve enough tough problems successfully to be useful even without common sense.

If their area of expertise is narrow, so is their focus. Expert systems plug away at one problem at a time. They ask questions of their users or obtain input from sensors and proceed from the data to some sort of conclusion. In one sense, an expert system is just one big transformation system, and the templates that its knowledge is expressed in are just rules of transformation. But the power of an expert system lies precisely in these rules. In order to do its job, an expert system needs to perform relatively few numerical calculations but a lot of symbolic processing. Symbolic processing implies that facts, observations, and hypotheses are represented by symbols and are manipulated as symbols. In other words, the expert system does not *know* in any sense what these symbols mean or stand for. Nevertheless, by these rules of transformation it is able to convert its input to some conclusion. That such a conclusion is meaningful and useful attests to the power of the technique. This manipulation is usually carried out by a computer, but there is no requirement that an expert system should be a computer program. Indeed, in tutorials on the subject one can demonstrate the workings of an expert system by asking the students to perform its actions; it is just faster, more accurate, and more convenient to implement it as a program.

So, in terms of essential characteristics, we can offer the following working definition:

> An *expert system* is a knowledge-based system that emulates expert thought to solve significant problems in a particular domain of expertise.

3.2 Desirable characteristics

Although our working definition gives what is essential to an expert system, practical expert systems must possess, in most cases, other characteristics if they are to be usable.

First of all an expert system must perform well on difficult problems. Mediocre performance would render it unreliable and performance restricted to easy problems would render it unemployable. But while the requirement is sensible, we must not take it to an extreme: it is not reasonable to expect better performance from an expert system than from an expert. If it turns out to be the case that our system does out-perform experts, that is an added bonus, not a rightful expectation. Of course, if we have implemented it on a computer, we can expect it to be available and fully functional for 24 hours a day, not to get tired, not to suffer from Monday morning blues or Friday afternoon impatience, and to give the same answer to beggars and kings. But we cannot rightfully expect that all its answers will always be correct, even less to demand a proof of their correctness. When we employ a human expert, we are given no such guarantees or proofs. We judge the tree by its fruit: if the expert does not perform well enough, we hire another; if the expert system does not perform well enough, we improve it. This has some important consequences concerning the responsibilities of those using expert systems, a point that we shall come back to in chapter 8.

The second practical requirement is that the system must be implementable. We observed earlier that the domain of an expert system is sharply focused. The reason for this is that at the moment the knowledge of even such a narrow domain requires a lot of effort to get hold of, to get into a working state, and to get right. Research is currently being conducted in this most pressing area of AI applications, in the area of *knowledge acquisition*. But until better methods are found, we have to strive for a rather fine balance: to keep the domain narrow enough to be implementable, yet wide enough to be useful.

The third requirement stems from the fact that expert systems interact with human beings: they ask questions, they deliver conclusions, they render advice. To do this effectively the system must converse in terms that the user can understand and in terms relevant to the problem at hand. This, however, is more an argument from virtue than necessity. As we can implement systems that observe this requirement relatively easily, there is no good reason for doing anything else. Nevertheless, it is an important factor when trying to persuade people to use the system, and it may become imperative if the situation in which the system is used demands swift user interaction.

The next requirement, however, is fundamental. Expert systems must be able to explain themselves, particularly in three respects. First of all, and most important, a system must be able to explain how it reached its conclusions from the facts given. If it cannot, there is no way to deal with conclusions that the user disagrees with. If it can, however, the explanation allows the user either to correct his own judgement of the case, or to reject that of the system; at least he is given enough information to do one or the other sensibly. The second, and sometimes equally important, requirement is for the system to be able to justify why it needs a particular piece of information. The user will want to know this in cases where to obtain the information is costly or - as can arise in a medical system - requires invasive or painful tests. Given such a facility, the user can judge the merit of each case and decide accordingly. The third requirement in this area is not an absolute one, but can be extremely useful. This is an ability on the part of the system to explain why it has not reached a particular conclusion, why it has not made a particular recommendation. This sort of explanation can sometimes be more illuminating than any other output.

Another important practical requirement is that these systems should work at the speed that the situation demands. This implies conversational pace for systems that talk to humans, real-time pace for systems that talk to other systems. This may appear too obvious a requirement to argue for, yet examples can be quoted of systems that were not adopted for serious use because they were too slow even for conversational use. So, if you wish to see your system in real use, make sure that it works at a speed that is commensurate with the problem and comfortable to its user.

There are also requirements placed on how the knowledge base should be implemented. Expert systems, like works of art, are never finished, merely abandoned. And they will be abandoned promptly if there is no easy way to modify and augment their knowledge base. Both our knowledge of a subject and our expectations of a system grow and change. If we cannot accommodate this growth and change, we end up with a fossilised product, a mere historical curiosity.

With respect to the methods of inference employed, there are two requirements. The first is that they should work. Now this may sound fatuous, but it will become more meaningful if we observe that studies of both MYCIN and PROSPECTOR have shown that they perform better than theoretical considerations should warrant. To put it succinctly, they seem to work in spite of the theory rather than because of it. But, the important fact is that they work. It is not the first time in the history of science that theory has had to catch up with practice. The second requirement is that enough methods of inference should be provided to allow expert rules to be expressed in a natural way. This is the requirement that systems offering only one method run counter to. As in any other walk of life, there are no universal cure-alls.

By now the message should be clear. Most of the above-stated practical requirements - implementability, modifiability, maintainability, response time, decent interface - are not unique to expert systems; they are all sound software engineering principles and, as such, represent nothing new or surprising. The outstanding special requirement is for an explanation facility. Because of its importance, many count this as an essential rather than just a desirable qualification.

3.3 Classification

There are several ways to classify expert systems. The first and most obvious way is by their area of application.

The most prolific area is medicine. Systems like MYCIN, INTERNIST, VM, PUFF, CASNET, KMS and MDX, all address medical specialties. There are two main reasons for such a wealth - some would say preponderance - of medical examples. One reason stems from the complexity of the underlying system, the human body. The need for expertise is especially acute when we try to deal with complex systems. The second reason is this: as we have studied this system longer and more intensely than any other, we have acquired a wealth of heuristic knowledge about its workings. And heuristics are the bread and butter of expert systems.

Chemistry and geology lead the field in other scientific areas: chemistry with DENDRAL, SECS, MOLGEN, and geology with PROSPECTOR and the Dipmeter Advisor.

Again, these are fields that appear to have qualified for inclusion by reasons of complexity and richness of heuristics.

Other applications come from a variety of fields, such as Rl from computer engineering, EL from electronics, and SACON from structural engineering. References to applications in education can also be seen, but not in the arts and humanities.

Another interesting, and perhaps more meaningful way of classifying expert systems is by the tasks that they are called upon to perform.

Some are called upon to analyse data and interpret its meaning. A good example is DENDRAL which interprets mass spectrometer data to determine the chemical structures that gave rise to it.

Others are asked to diagnose the reasons for or sources of disparity between expected and actual states or operations of a system. Medical and machine diagnostic programs like MYCIN and DART I come into this category.

Some have as their main task to predict the next state or action of a system on the basis of data from its current state, specifically to give warning of impending malfunction. Although there are several systems built to carry out tasks in this category - such as machine monitoring, economic and political risk analysis for expanding multi-nationals - the only one reported in the literature is VM.

Some systems were built to perform all the above tasks - analysis, diagnosis, prognosis - and to finish off the consultation with a recommended treatment. The shining example is MYCIN. These tasks, as MYCIN shows, form a natural progression, but not all systems are required to proceed all the way from analysis to treatment.

There is yet another, very useful task: teaching. Expert systems embody knowledge of their domain; this knowledge can be used to train new experts. This is the task of GUIDON, namely to teach medical students how to diagnose and treat blood diseases, on the basis of MYCIN's knowledge base.

Obviously, there are countless other ways in which expert systems could be classified, but the two that we have seen are probably the most important.

Questions

1. Given a program that advises budding Modigliani's on where to put what size rectangles on the canvas and how to colour them, on the basis of random selection, would you class it as an expert system? If its selection were guided by rules of composition and colour harmony, would that make it an expert system?

2. Consider BELLE, the strongest chess-playing program today. It is said to have an ELO rating of over 2000, which means that it would beat 95 per cent of chess players. It generates a possible-moves tree and evaluates the resulting positions, assisted by powerful tree-pruning and cutoff heuristics. Would you say that it was an expert system? A knowledge-based system?

4   Creation

4.1 How expert systems are built

4.1.1 Unique features of the life cycle

Having gained an understanding of expert systems, we can now turn to how they are implemented. In common with conventional computer systems, expert systems are created, used, modified, re-used, and eventually discarded in much the same way as any other system. To the software engineer they are just another piece of software and subject to the same disciplines. But they also show marked differences in most phases of their life-cycle. When conceiving likely applications, we need to match suitability of the problem with feasibility of the technique as applied to the problem. This can be a difficult problem, which we shall return to in chapter 8.

Having passed the first hurdle and identified a likely application, we find that to implement an expert system brings its own difficulties. To overcome them, we need not only all our know-how in software engineering but also additional techniques. The reason for this is easy to see: expert systems are made up of conventional software items together with unique components.

An expert system is essentially composed of a knowledge base, a database, an inference engine, and some support software. The central part is the inference engine. The *knowledge base* holds whatever information we have found appropriate to solving problems on our chosen domain. It is specific to the particular application. The *database* is the work area of the system. The *support software* provides the interface to the environment. The *inference engine*, as its name implies, provides the motive power to the system. Its functions are: to determine what data it needs to solve the problem at hand, to get this data via the support software, to lodge it in the database, to employ the contents of the the knowledge base to draw inferences, and to record these as well in the database. It exercises these functions repeatedly, until it can do, or need do, no more.

In this chapter we shall look at some important issues in implementation. Having implemented the system, we need to convince ourselves of its accuracy and validity. This, again, is a task that comes naturally to software engineers, but one that presents unique problems in expert systems. We shall examine these problems in chapter 6.

Finally, to round up the differences between expert and conventional systems, expert systems show a far greater propensity to change than others and, as a consequence, demand modifications to be made more frequently. We will look at this aspect in chapter 8.

4.1.2 Developing the system

Developing an expert system is, in many ways, just developing a piece of software. It becomes subject, therefore, to the same engineering disciplines, methods and techniques as other software. This may seem platitudinous, but needs stating nevertheless. A number of systems were built without these practices. The consequences were predictable: these systems are shaky, difficult to modify and maintain; they present an awkward user interface, ignore resource management mandates - in short, the usual consequences of inadequate engineering. This is not meant as a criticism of the early systems. They were not created for commercial or industrial use: they were built to test and develop an idea. But the systems that we are called upon to build are no longer research vehicles, designed to prove the feasibility of an idea; they are there to be used in earnest. We must, therefore, pay close attention to proper engineering or else accept the risk of dissatisfied users.

4.1.3 Manpower requirements

Developing an expert system is a software engineering project, so our first task is to look at the likely resource requirements. We shall look at the three major resources - manpower, machinery, and time - in turn.

There are two aspects to the question of manpower: how much do we need and what skills are required.

Manpower needs are difficult to quantify as they are almost totally application-dependent, not only on the area of application but also on the depth and capabilities required of the system. Expert systems have been built by people working on their own and also by sizeable teams. How many staff we need depends also on how quickly we want the system (bearing in mind the gestation limit, as in the well-known engineer's saying: Nine women cannot produce one baby in one month). It also depends on how many different roles individuals on the team can fill.

This leads us naturally to the question of the necessary roles. In conventional systems we are used to seeing analysts, designers, and programmers; in our systems we need similar but somewhat different roles. We, too, need someone to carry out the analysis functions, but we call him a *knowledge engineer*. He assumes the mantle of the analyst and, to some extent, that of the designer. His role is to decide whether the proposed system is feasible, and how it should be implemented. He is also given the tasks of gathering the knowledge that makes up the knowledge base and of bringing it to a workable state. In addition, he has to make sure that the system is usable and safe, and that it fulfils its intended objectives.

The second major role - he has not yet been given a new name - is that of the implementor. Just as the knowledge engineer straddles the roles of the analyst and the designer, so the implementor assumes the responsibilities of the designer and the programmer. Whereas the knowledge engineer makes major, strategic decisions, the implementor makes minor, tactical ones. It is his job to program the system and to validate it as a piece of software (validating it as an expert system is the knowledge engineer's responsibility).

The third role is unique to expert systems, namely that of the domain expert. Without expertise there can be no expert system; so this role is not only unique but also vital. We shall examine this role in section 4.2.

Thus we have three different roles to fill: the knowledge engineer, the implementor and the domain expert. Rarely can one person effectively carry out more than one of these roles. Equally rare to find is a large team.

4.1.4 Machine requirements

Machine requirements show wide variations. Some systems run on personal computers, some on minicomputers, some on mainframes. Obviously, large and complex *models* - as knowledge engineers call the domain-specific parts - need larger hardware, while modest ones make do with smaller. This much they hold in common with conventional systems; where they differ is in their demands for specific hardware resources.

Expert system have a voracious appetite for memory. Whether this is primary or backing storage depends on the type of system.

Conversational systems handle large amounts of text. Because they tend to be used as advisors to people, they need to talk to their clients in an understandable fashion. The nearer what they display is to natural language, the more characters it demands - natural language being highly redundant. The more help they provide, the more fully they explain their actions; the more precisely they cast their questions, and the more they expand on their conclusions, the more text they need to store. But as only small sections are needed at any one time, text can be kept on backing storage. As a rough guide, we need to reserve for this text in an average system about 1M bytes of backing storage.

In comparison, the primary storage requirements can be more modest. Several systems make do with as little as 64K bytes of address space. But this figure very much depends on the programming language used and on the run-time support that it provides. A system implemented in Pascal will need less space than the same system written in Interlisp.

There are, of course, systems that are other than conversational. For example, some continuously monitor equipment, while others are embedded in conventional systems. Their storage requirements vary widely. In general, they need more primary storage but less secondary storage than conversational systems. They are sufficiently diverse, however, to make generalisations difficult.

A similarly wide divergence of needs can be observed when we look at processing power. Conversational systems need to run only at human speeds, and even microcomputers can cope with that. But system embedded in real-time applications show a voracious appetite for CPU cycles. So much so, it is safe to say, that these applications outrun the capabilities of most machines, and their designers eagerly await faster processors and other hardware, specifically tailored to their needs.

In summary, the hardware requirements of the type of system that we are mainly concerned with in this book, namely conversational expert systems, have modest enough processor requirements so that they can be mounted on a business microcomputer, but usually need more backing storage than is normally available on these machines.

One further aspect of software implementation that we need to look at is what languages and other tools we need to build expert systems. This is a much-debated subject, and at the moment the debate generates more heat than light. Fortunately for us, there is also a lot of accumulated experience to guide us.

The first choice that we have to make is how to implement our system. We have two options: we can provide all the necessary functions ourselves, or we can use an expert system *shell*. The first approach implements the system, from the ground up, using our favourite programming language and environment. So far, the language used by AI researchers has tended to be LISP, occasionally and latterly also PROLOG. The debate on the relative merits of these two languages occupies more space in the journals and takes more time of researchers than it deserves. All we need to note is that systems have been created using either of these languages and, if you have access to one and not the other, or you feel more at home with one than the other, the question is largely academic. Furthermore, LISP and PROLOG are not the only alternatives: several systems have been implemented using conventional programming languages such as Pascal or FORTRAN. Our choice must be governed by pragmatic considerations.

A far more important choice to make is whether to use an expert system building tool or *shell*. There are several available. Some come from universities and are outgrowths of specific expert systems. The best-known examples of these are EMYCIN (developed from MYCIN), KAS (from PROSPECTOR), and EXPERT (from CASNET). Others have been specially created to ease the job of the knowledge engineer, packages like ROSIE, OPS, RLL, and AGE. But if the universities are busy providing us with tools, so is industry. The number of

commercially marked expert system shells is
constantly growing. Using these shells or packages has
the obvious advantage that we have less to implement.
They give us a ready-to-run system which needs only the
domain-specific parts to be added. They, typically,
provide tools to ease the task of adding those parts in
the form of rule editors and diagnostic aids. Even more
important, they can provide us with a way to think
about the problem as well as a method for solving it:
a good set of tools has prescriptive as well as
descriptive power; thus they can become not only tools
of convenience but also tools of thought.

4.1.5 Time

There is, as yet, not enough accumulated experience to
give us reliable estimators for how much time we should
allow to develop these systems. The task is made more
than usually difficult by the fact that, as knowledge
never stays static for a long time, knowledge bases
tend to need constant updating. Consequently, the dates
of project completions are very hazy. Predictably,
projects using shells and knowledge engineering aids
progress faster than others. But most time is always
spent on building and verifying the knowledge base.
This brings us conveniently to the topic of the next
section.

4.2 Knowledge acquisition

Having looked at expert systems through the eyes of a
software engineer, we can now turn our attention to two
problems specific to them, both stemming from the fact
that these systems incorporate knowledge. One is the
problem of how to obtain this knowledge, or the problem
of *knowledge acquisition*; the other is how to encode
and store this knowledge, or the problem of *knowledge
representation*.

4.2.1 Building the knowledge base

Knowledge acquisition is the process of building the
knowledge content of expert systems, the so-called
knowledge base. It is a process that carries on
throughout the life of the system. It has several tasks

to perform: it has to elicit knowledge, organise it, encode it, validate it and tune it.

Elicitation must carry out several operations, the most important of which are the following:

1. Extracting the knowledge by externalising it and thus making it available for inspection and manipulation.
2. Rendering it explicit by accumulating sufficient detail to make it clear and give it full expression.
3. Recording it in symbolic form.
4. Verifying it by checking the symbolic form against the original statement and intention.

Elicitation delivers single items of knowledge that need to be organised into a unified whole. How much organising is needed depends very much on the way in which the knowledge base is implemented and used. Some implementations require items to be arranged in groups and sequences, where the arrangement displays relationships between items in the knowledge base. Their order could be used, for example, to determine the sequence in which various items are used - an important decision that the system has to make if several items could be validly used at a certain point of consultation. To quote a concrete example, many systems need a certain set of information about the client or patient: name, age, sex, etc. The system has to choose in what order to obtain this information. A simple way to make this choice is to follow the textual order of these items in the knowledge base. In other cases it may be essential that, even though several items could be used, they are used in a set order of priority. Again, textual order could be one way to define their relative priorities.

Having obtained the information and having organised it, we still need to make it available to the system. This usually implies some form of coding. Knowledge bases are usually encoded in two different forms: one external, one internal. The external one is human readable and serves human needs, the internal is cast in a form more suitable for the machine and this one serves efficiency needs. The two are, in most cases, different: what may be convenient for us may not be the best form to access and process. Ideally, the knowledge engineer should need to prepare only the external form, the internal one being produced automatically, usually by a compiler (see also section 4.4).

4.2.2 Sources of knowledge

We have three main sources of knowledge: literature, experts and examples. And we have three different bases of knowledge: scientific laws, experience and models. Chapter 3 stipulated that knowledge for our purposes is anny information that helps us to solve problems in the domain. The most helpful information is an expression of some regularity that allows us to predict what will happen next or to explain how and why something has happened. The strongest forms of regularity that we know are the laws of science. Consequently, acquiring knowledge in a scientific subject is much easier than in any other field, and it matters little whether we get these laws from a book or from an expert. In other, scientifically weaker domains, the regularities that we are after are weaker and often not clearly expressed. We do not speak of 'laws' in gardening or advising investors, nevertheless the expert in these fields is aware of many interesting regularities and uses them daily. Here the question of source becomes more acute. In the practical - or at least scientifically weak - fields, experts' experience may not codified and written down. We need a live expert simply because little is available in written form. The majority of expert system applications so far have been in these areas; they rely on accumulated wealth of experience, but lack scientific formulation. The greatest difficulty when collecting data in these fields is that the expert may not be able to verbalise the knowledge that he uses. This is what makes knowledge acquisition often a difficult and frustrating task for both the expert and the knowledge engineer. Still, systems have been built and will be built in just this way.
    Some AI researchers, frustrated by this rather error-prone and protracted process, have tried to devise different methods for obtaining knowledge. Their main criticism of knowledge acquisition by interviewing experts is that it misuses the experts' capabilities. They argue that what we ask of the expert is not what he is necessarily good at: definitions, hypotheses, laws. Often the expert is not even aware of the rules by which he solves a problem; his knowledge exists at a subconcious level. It would be to both party's

advantage, the claim goes, if we used experts for what they are good at, namely generating or scrutinising examples.

Given a database of examples, we can employ a new technique: induction. This is the only automatic method at the moment that we can use for knowledge acquisition. It has been successfully employed, for example, to create an expert system that diagnoses soya bean diseases. This is an active field of research in AI - mechanised knowledge acquisition - and of immense importance. But at the moment, most knowledge-based systems are built using interviewing and literature search techniques.

In scientific fields, knowledge acquisition is relatively easy because of the existence of scientific laws. This, unfortunately, is only strictly true for the 'hard' disciplines, in other words for those which have managed to establish verified laws, hypotheses and models of their domain. In all other disciplines knowledge acquisition is made easier if the discipline employs scientific method and has advanced beyond the stage of being a merely descriptive science. It is a fact, though, that those applications for which we are most anxious to build expert systems come from precisely the scientifically weak - or even non-scientific - fields. Here we do not have verified laws or models, and the knowledge that we use to solve problems is based on experience and observation only. This type of knowledge, although it can be extremely useful, suffers from two drawbacks. First of all, it is very difficult to get hold of and formulate, and may be impossible to verify. Secondly, unlike scientific laws, these empirical, heuristic rules do not have the power of laws: they are, almost without exception, partial; and we have to take great care in establishing the limits of their applicability. The designation 'partial' can mean one of two things. They are either not applicable in all cases, or they can only deliver probabilistic indications. The rule 'if you go out in the rain you will get wet' can have many exceptions, and if we wish to use this rule in a system, we have to build those exceptions in as well. A diagnostic rule like 'spots indicate chickenpox' gives us only an indication of likelihood, not of certainty, and this degree of likelihood has to be similarly made explicit in the system.

The next difficult question to tackle is just what does knowledge acquisition collect. We are after three different sorts of knowledge. The first is the simplest, and goes by the name of *perceptual knowledge*. This covers knowledge of simple facts and relationships, like the colour of quartz crystals, the Curie temperature of iron, or the maximum torque of an engine. Strictly speaking, expert systems do not need to hold these items, because they could be obtained as answers to questions. But most users would find questions of this sort highly irritating, which in turn could reduce their willingness to use the system. The next level up we find what most people would consider knowledge: concepts and relationships. Here we find scientific laws like Maxwell's equations and Boyle's Law. We also find heuristic observations like 'fever indicates illness'. This is meat and drink to expert systems. But there is a third and extremely important level. Experts bring to bear on a problem not only their scientific knowledge and their experience, but also knowledge of how to set about a problem, how to go round difficulties, what else to try when they get stuck. This could be termed an expert's *strategic knowledge*. The effectiveness of expert systems can depend to a great extent on how good their strategic knowledge base is. The three levels indicate not only the power of these items but also how difficult they are to get hold of. Perceptual knowledge is the easiest, strategic the hardest. The levels also indicate their importance and usefulness.

There are other ways of classifying knowledge, but only one more is important to the knowledge engineer. That is the division of knowledge into those aspects that help us to solve problems and those that give advice. The first type helps us to classify and to diagnose; in general, this is knowledge that proceeds from the given to some conclusion. It is this type of knowledge that the car mechanic uses to establish why a car will not start. The second class proceeds from the conclusions of the first to practical statements. This is the knowledge that allows the car mechanic to repair the car so that it will start. The distinction is important to the knowledge engineer because it allows him to structure the knowledge base and, through that, decide on the order that the system should follow in its operations. Advice usually follows diagnosis and classification.

It would be useful if we could close this section with practical advice on how to acquire knowledge. Unfortunately, there is no science of knowledge

acquisition. It could hardly even be called a
discipline. What advice is available tends to be *ad
hoc* and often no more than common sense. Many of the
proposed methods appear to work only for some
individuals or in some cases. The most useful advice is
that it should be tackled like a project: we should
start by establishing the objectives of the proposed
system. From these objectives we can then derive the
top level conclusions - and the accompanying advice -
for the system. Next, we should establish what
information can be made available as input. What
follows thereafter is a mixture of working backwards
from the conclusions and working forward from the
inputs. Most people's experience is that working
backwards is often easier and almost always more
reliable. In this direction we can establish the
deductive path to the conclusions and what information
we need to start on those paths. This can be safer and
more productive, because it establishes what
information is needed to solve the problem rather than
asking the question 'What shall I do with the
information I have?' (In most applications we find that
this information requirement analysis is done for the
first time when collecting knowledge for an expert
system. It often comes as a shock to the users of the
current system to find that the information that they
have is either insufficient or of the wrong kind. This
is such a desirable side-effect that the analysis work
is justified even if there is not going to be an expert
system at the end of it.)

4.3 Knowledge representation

When we collect knowledge, we are faced with the
problem of how to record it. And when we try to build
the knowledge base we have the similar problem of how
to represent it. We could just write down what we are
told but, as the information grows, it becomes more and
more difficult to keep track of the relationships
between the items. And the written word is not the best
way to represent this knowledge to the machine.

Let us start with the observation that we have no
perfect method of knowledge representation today. This
stems largely from our ignorance of just what knowledge
is. Nevertheless, many methods have been worked out and
used by AI researchers, and we shall examine some of
these.

There are two fundamentally different methods of representing knowledge: as program, which we call *procedural*, and as data, which we call *declarative*. Early representation schemes - such as the scheme used by GPS, for example - were predominantly procedural; they were the natural outgrowth of traditional programming and had the outstanding advantage of being highly efficient, which in those days meant barely executable within a reasonable time. This method still retains its advantage. Nevertheless, with the increase of computing power, some researchers turned to declarative representation. When the method was first conceived, a long and often lively debate ensued on the relative merits of the two. The debate was never resolved, it merely lost prominence. The AI community now recognises that each has its place, adopts a 'horses for courses' attitude, and debates more important and more interesting issues.

Some of the more important arguments are nevertheless worth reviewing. The main sources of dissatisfaction with procedural encoding were the following: because knowledge is embedded in code, the representation is rather opaque; its meaning is not only hard to perceive but also suffers from the ills of conventional procedures, especially from being context-dependent; and the combined effects of opacity and context-dependence render these systems hard to understand and hard to modify. On the other hand, declarative encoding records knowledge as data and is, therefore, less heavily encoded and more understandable. Ease of understanding leads to ease of modification, as data is easier to modify than programs. And, above all, data is context-independent.

The semantics, the meaning of procedurally encoded knowledge, is distributed over all the procedures. In declarative encoding the semantics are lodged in a few procedures which are used globally. Thus the semantics are gathered in one place and are homogeneous. On the other hand, procedural encoding brings faster execution; the difference being analogous to the difference between compiled and interpreted code. Furthermore, in procedural encoding the programmer has full control over the progress of the system, whereas declarative schemes relinquish control to the state of the system and the semantic routines; this can be very difficult to predict and control.

The combined benefits of ease of understanding, ease of modification, and semantic clarity - even at the expense of slower execution speed and a certain loss of control - have been found to be too important to do without in expert systems. Consequently, most of these systems employ some form of declarative representation.

There are many forms of declarative representation that we could choose: propositional logic, predicate logic, semantic networks, analogue representations, frames, semantic triples, production rules, to mention but a few. Barr and Feigenbaum's Handbook gives a good overview of these schemes and of their relative merits. However, the two schemes that have found favour with expert system builders are semantic networks and production rules.

The semantic network used in PROSPECTOR is a directed acyclic graph. The nodes in this graph represent expressions that deliver values. The terms of the expressions are indicated by the arcs pointing from other nodes to the expression node. The leaf nodes represent data, either stored in the knowledge base or obtained as answers to questions. The operators in the expressions are the operators of fuzzy logic or of Bayesian inference. For a thorough examination of semantic networks the reader should consult Nilsson's *Principles of Artificial Intelligence*.

Semantic networks are powerful. In fact, proof exists that they are *Turing complete*, which means that anything we can do on a Turing machine, we can achieve using semantic nets.

The second popular representation is *production rules*. Production rules are a development of *production systems*, a formalism proposed by Emil Post in 1943. We know that his system is also Turing complete (see Minsky's *Computation: Finite and Infinite Machines* (1967) and Anderson's *Language, Memory and Thought* (1974) for formal proofs). We can, therefore, rest assured that they are computationally powerful enough. Newell and Simon's *Human Problem Solving* (1972) made a strong case for their conjecture that production systems model closely human cognitive processes. If their conjecture is correct, this would argue strongly for the suitability in systems that emulate human thought. Their claim is certainly justified in view of the successes of the systems built on this formalism. The best known example of such a system is MYCIN, but there are many others. The scheme also has the added advantage in that it does not completely rule out the possibility - and hence the advantages of - procedural encoding. On the contrary, it provides a workable bridge between the two methods. We shall make use of this formalism for our prototypes, but only as a declarative method.

Davis and King's monograph in *Machine Intelligence 8* (1977) provide an excellent overview and evaluation of production systems. We shall touch on only the most important aspects. The most accessible way to view them is as a set of conditional statements (the *rules*), a collection of given or derived facts (the *database*), and an interpreter that implements the invocation of these rules as a sequence of *modus ponens* actions.

The rules are *condition-action* pairs. The interpreter evaluates the conditions with reference to the database of facts and, if successful in fulfilling the condition, performs the action. As the interpreter does this repeatedly, its action is referred to as the *recognise-act cycle*. Success in fulfilling the condition can be established at various levels of sophistication ranging from simple identity (literal match), through matching expression over literals allowing variables on the left-hand side (pattern matching), up to allowing variables on both sides (unification). Let us suppose, for example, that some of the rules are

if it is raining then the ground is wet
if height of X > height of Y then X is taller than Y

where X and Y are variables, and the database has the following items:

it is raining
the ground is dry
height of Tom = 6
height of Tim = 5
Tom is taller than Y

A literal match would satisfy the first rule; 'it is raining' in the database matches exactly the condition part of the rule. Pattern matching could satisfy the second rule by letting X take the value 'Tom' and Y the value 'Tim'. The last item in the database – which effectively makes the claim that Tom is taller than anyone – would allow the system to fulfil the condition of the second rule by unification, letting X take the value 'Tom'. We shall use expressions over literals, this being the most commonly used form.

The simplest action is replacement; this replaces an old item in the database with a new one. In the example above, 'the ground is dry' would be replaced by 'the ground is wet'. The next level up is addition; this aggregates items in the database. This is the most frequently used action. In our example the system could add 'Tom is taller than Tim' to the database. And if it used unification, it could add 'height of Tom > height of Y'. More complex actions are conceivable and have, indeed, been used, such as calling procedures and depositing markers which will invoke other rules, etc. The chief merit of the straightforward addition scheme is that it preserves ease of modifiability. It does so in the sense that rules can be added or changed independently of other rules, that is, in the expectation that other rules will not have to be changed as a result. With more complex action schemes, this may not be the case.

4.4 Internal representation and the compiler

As we saw earlier, the system's knowledge is best represented in two different forms: an external form for human consumption and an internal one for the machine. We also saw that, ideally, the internal form should be produced automatically rather than by hand. As the representation must, in this case, adhere to some syntactic form, this conversion is a job for a compiler. Representation languages show a simple syntax, consequently writing the compiler is straightforward. There are a number of excellent books on compiler writing - one of the best and most practical appears in the same series as this book, Bornat's *Understanding and Writing Compilers*, (1979) - so we shall not dwell on technical issues relating to compiler writing.

There are, however, additional services that these compilers can render. They can provide a number of useful checks that help the job of a knowledge engineer. The first of these is a check that there are no contradictory rules in the knowledge base. Stated precisely, what the compiler should check for is that there are no two rules that have the same condition parts but that result in opposing actions, such as depositing contradictory items of information in the database. For example, this bars two rules of the form

if a then c   and   if a then ~c

both appearing in the rule base.

The second is a check against circularity, which ensures that there is no rule such that it requires its own action to establish its own condition, whether directly or through the exercise of other rules. Thus it will, for example, check that no chain of rules of the form

```
if a  then c1
if c1 then c2
   :
if cn then a
```

can be found. It must be stated, though, that this is a contentious issue. Several systems allow circular reasoning, and take precautions to prevent the system from looping. Whether or not we need circular reasoning to build expert systems, is an open question. Logicians react strongly against any such claim, but several practitioners demand the facility.

The compiler can save a lot of work in preparing the knowledge base. It can, for example, check that the rules are properly connected such that there are no 'unreachable' rules or that all constants used are properly declared. All in all, a good compiler can not only give us a more efficient system but also the means to produce it more efficiently.

Further reading

William J. van Melle describes EMYCIN in great detail in *System Aids in Constructing Consultation Programs* (UMI Research Press, 1981).

An overview of languages and tools for knowledge engineering is chapter 9 in F. Hayes-Roth, D.A. Waterman and D.B. Lenat's *Building Expert Systems* (Addison-Wesley, 1983). They discuss EMYCIN, KAS, EXPERT, OPS5, RLL, ROSIE and AGE.

Avron Barr and Edward Feigenbaum's three volume compendium, *The Handbook of Artificial Intelligence* (Pitman, 1981-3) is a rich source of very accessible material on various aspects of AI. Volume I devotes an entire chapter to knowledge repesentation. In Volume II you will find a section on EXPERT.

Probably the best description and analysis of semantic nets is chapter 9 in Nils Nilsson's book, *Principles of Artificial Intelligence* (Springer-Verlag, 1982).

Emil Post's paper 'Formal reductions of the general combinatorial decision problem' appeared in *American Journal of Mathematics*, Vol. 65 (1943). Marvin Minsky describes its essential ideas and gives the proof for Turing completeness in *Computation: Finite and Infinite Machines* (Prentice-Hall, 1967), as does J. Anderson in *Language, Memory and Thought* (Erlbaum Associates, 1976).

Allen Newell and Herbert Simon's *Human Problem Solving* (Prentice-Hall, 1972) is an in-depth examination of how we use productions to tackle problems. It is worth reading not only for the theory it propounds, but also for the wealth of example rules and production systems.

R. Davis and J. King's monograph, 'An overview of production systems' appeared in E.W. Elcock and D. Michie (eds), *Machine Intelligence 8* (Ellis Horwood, 1977).

Richard Bornat's excellent book, *Understanding and Writing Compilers* (Macmillan, 1979) is full of practical advice for compiler writers.

5 Operation

5.1 The basics

In this chapter we are going to examine how an expert system operates. We will look at the major functions in detail, at the programming level. The reason for descending to such a detailed level is not because the algorithms are unusual or inherently difficult. On the contrary, the reason is to show that they are not. Nevertheless, so as not to lose sight of fundamental ideas, we will start with a very simple - and inadequate - formulation and elaborate on it.

It is relatively straightforward to develop a skeletal expert system if we restrict ourselves to the basic functions lying at the heart of such systems and if we use well tried and tested methods of implementation. But what are these basic functions and facilities that we need to provide? In Chapter 4 we considered the options open to us in terms of knowledge encoding and representation. The advantages of declarative encoding appear to be more important than speed and, of the various representation schemes, production rules are not only the most used, but also the best tried and tested.

If we examine how we solve problems through rules, be it rules from a discipline or rules of thumb, we can discern three fundamental elements: knowledge consisting of conditional statements, data obtained from the problem at hand, and the process of inference. We observe, for example, that our car's engine idles badly and even stalls, but only in cold weather. An experienced mechanic will tell us that the choke is likely to be at fault. If we ask him for his reasons for coming to this conclusion, he will tell us that those are the classic signs of a choke misbehaving. Much of his knowledge consists of such symptom/fault pairs. And, having acquired such knowledge through learning and experience, all that he needs to do is to find a suitable pair whose symptom half matches the problem at hand. Having found it, he applies a simple rule of inference and takes himself a step nearer to the solution of the problem.

The power of an expert system - like that of an expert - comes from its store of patterns and some method of employing those patterns to solve problems. A generalisation of the symptom/fault type patterns is the *conditional* (or *rule*). A conditional has two parts, an *antecedent* (or *condition*) and a *consequent* (or *conclusion*, or *action*). The system progresses by inferring the consequent whenever the antecedents match the problem at hand. This is the simplest and most fundamental rule of inference; it was known and decribed by Aristotle, and stood us in good stead for over 2000 years. It is the rule of *modus ponens*. The schema for it is simply

```
from     if p then q
and      p
infer    q
```

This gives us a useful agenda: to implement an expert system we must create some mechanism

for recording conditionals relevant to the domain
for obtaining information about the problem
for applying the conditionals to the information and
for communicating the results to the user.

The rule of *modus ponens*, however, does not tell us how to set about solving a problem; it does not tell us where to start and how to proceed. Apart from a rule of inference, we need in addition some principle of strategy. There are two strategies that have also long been employed in logic and mathematics:

1. We can work forward from the given to the conclusion. This mode of proceeding answers the question: What can we conclude from the given data?
2. Or we can work backwards (as long as we ′ where we want to end up, of course) fr hypothesis to the data supporting it. ′ answers the question: Can we prove the from the given data?

This, then, gives us the two fundamental strategies for expert systems, known as *forward chaining* and *backward chaining*.

5.2 Forward chainer

Let us see how we can implement this *modus ponens* engine, using the two different strategies. In this section we build a forward chainer. First we need to establish the data structures that we need and how we make use of them.

We need some notation to present our algorithms. As our requirements are modest, we do not need the power of a full language, just a few constructs. Furthermore, as our interest is mainly in what the algorithms do rather than in how they do it, we present them in a simplified form as far as possible. In this form, the algorithms will be presented as a set of definitions. The definition of a function takes the following form

let *function-name(arguments)* = *body*

The body of a function can be a series of function calls, commands, if-statements, for-statements, or loop-statements. If there is more than one call, command or expression, we shall enclose the series between braces { ... }. The form of an if-statement is

if *condition* **then** *body*
else if *condition* **then** *body*
    :
else *body*

Conditions can be function calls or boolean expressions on function calls using the boolean operators **not,** **and,** **or.** The form of a for-statement is

for each *variable* **in** *list*
until *condition*
body

This statement declares a *variable* ranging over the members of *list*, either all members - if the

until part is omitted - or until the *condition* is attained. The form of a loop-statement is

loop *body* **until** *condition*

The *body* of this statement will be repeatedly executed until the *condition* is achieved. We use print-commands to produce our output and a set-command for assignment. Their forms are

print(item)
printlist(list)
set *variable = expression*

Within a *body*, we can also make local definitions in a form similar to a function definition

let *name = body*

The scope of these definitions is the body, enclosed in braces, containing the definition. Our basic data structure is the list handled by the use of the usual list functions such as *null(x)*, *head(x)*, *tail(x)*, *cons(x,y)*, *member(x,y)*, and *append(x,y)*. The predicate *null(x)* is true if *x* is empty; *head(x)* delivers the first item of a non-empty list, and *tail(x)* what remains; *cons(x,y)* makes a new list composed of the item *x* and the list *y*; *member(x,y)* is true if *x* is in the list *y*; *append(x,y)* makes a new list by adding the item *x* to the end of the list *y*.

The rule base is a list of rules. Our rules have two parts: a list of antecedents and a list of consequents. We can access these lists in a rule *r* through the selectors *antecedents(r)* and *consequents(r)*. The database is a list of facts.

Using these facilities we can express one possible algorithm for the forward chainer as in (5.1).

Its operation can be explained simply as follows: given a list of rules, the forward chainer attempts to draw all possible conclusions. It starts by examining the rules that it is given; if it finds no further rules to consider, it exits with the conclusions found - the list *facts* - which also include the original data given to it. If there are more rules to consider, it takes the first one. If the first one cannot fire, it recurses on the rest of the rules. If the rule does fire, the new facts that it contributes are accumulated in *new*. If no new facts can be found, the forward chainer recurses on the rest of the rules. But if there are some new facts, these are added to the database, and the forward chainer restarts with all the rules and the new database.

```
let forward(ruleset,facts) =                          (5.1)
{ if null(ruleset) then facts
  else
  { let r=head(ruleset)
    if not doesfire(r)
    then forward(tail(ruleset),facts)
    else
    { let new=canuse(r)
      if null(new)
      then forward(tail(ruleset),facts)
      else forward(rules,append(new,facts))
    } } }
```

It uses some help functions. The function *doesfire(r)* (5.2) tests whether a rule *r* can fire or not. A rule can fire if all its antecedents are in the database.

```
let doesfire(r) = listand(antecedents(r))            (5.2)
```

```
let listand(s) =
{ if null(s) then true
  else if member(head(s),facts)
  then listand(tail(s))
  else false }
```

The function *canuse(r)* (5.3) accumulates all the new facts that the rule *r* can contribute. We can employ the method of handing its job to another function with an accumulator parameter, in this case *usesome(cs,u)*. This will add a fact to the list *u* if it is not already in the database.

```
let canuse(r) = usesome(consequents(r),nil)          (5.3)
```

```
let usesome(cs,u) =
{ if null(cs) then u
  else
  { let x=head(cs)
    if member(x,facts) then usesome(tail(cs),u)
    else usesome(tail(cs),cons(x,u)) } }
```

We can invoke the forward chainer something like this:

```
let inf = forward(rules,data)
print("I can infer that:")
printlist(inf)
```

The main use of a forward chainer would be in an embedded, rather than a conversational, system. By an *embedded* expert system we mean one that is part of a larger, conventional system; in this form the expert system provides those functions that the designers wanted to be knowledge based while other functions are provided by conventional techniques. Why is a forward chainer a particularly suitable form for implementing embedded expert systems? The main reason is that it makes a fundamental assumption, namely that all the information that it will need - or is ever likely to be given - will be available at the start and as one set. This sort of situation is far more likely to arise when it is used as part of some larger system. Conversely, it is not likely to arise in a conversational, interactive system. Users like to be prompted for data so that they do not have to worry about what order to input it or about the risk of omitting something.

Given that the forward chainer is more useful in an embedded form, although we may have a good specification, to implement it as we have done here would be bad engineering. If we can impose a limitation, we can do much better. The limitation is that we do not allow circular reasoning. For example, we do not allow three rules of the form 'if a then b', 'if b then c', and 'if c then a'. Although one can imagine situations in which circular reasoning would be useful, the restriction is not too onerous. Perhaps the best way to illustrate this is through an example.

Let us take the case of trying to simulate, through the use of rules, a feedback situation. For example, let us try to simulate a potentially dangerous positive feedback in a transistor circuit. We have the following rules

```
if the collector current increases
then the junction temperature will rise

if the junction temperature rises
then the leakage current will rise
```

if the leakage current rises
then the collector current will increase

These rules describe the unfortunate behaviour in an unprotected transistor circuit. Their idea is that when we detect a rise in the collector current, we follow the feedback loop round several times until the base temperature gets to a dangerous level and the transistor destroys itself. However, this is only one way of stating the rules. This formulation views the system at one particular level, namely the lowest. In contrast, when we ask an electronics expert about the likely behaviour of this circuit, he will tell us that it is unsafe because it will suffer from thermal runaway. If we ask him to explain his reasoning, he will tell us that he deduced this from the fact that the circuit is unprotected. His reasoning will not go round and round until some disaster befalls the transistor. The unstated rule he uses is something like this:

if there is no protective circuit then
the transistor will be destroyed by thermal runaway

The purpose of this example is to illustrate the conjecture that circular reasoning can be replaced by some rules that go directly from cause to effect. The corollary to this is that if we can state the cause and effect link in this way, we have no need of circular rules. So, there are cases that can live with the restriction.

If the conjecture holds, we have a much better way of implementing our forward chainer. If we look upon the rules as directed arcs from antecedents to consequents, the rule set can be cast as a directed acyclic graph or DAG. This DAG can be compiled into a set sequence of operations which access only relevant rules at any time (instead of all rules all the time, as our forward chainer does) and it carries out operations only if they are called for and only once. Hence it can execute at a much higher speed - a most desirable characteristic for an embedded system.

Our main interest, however, is not in embedded, but in interactive, advisory systems. As a consequence, we shall say no more about forward chaining systems. Nevertheless, additional facilities, such as those that we shall add to backward chainers and that would be useful for forward chainers, can be added in an analogous fashion.

5.3 The basic backward chainer

Using the same data structures and basic functions as for the forward chainer, we can implement a simple backward chainer. As we saw under the description of the two strategies, the backward chainer starts with the top hypotheses or *goals* and tries to confirm or refute them. The goals, just like the rules, are domain-specific, and need to be stated. In most systems they form part of the rule base, that is the static data structure. As we shall see, however, when chaining back from goals, subgoals are established which can be treated in much the same way as the top goals. It is for this reason that the goals that we ask the system to work on are given as the parameter to the backchainer.

The backward chainer (5.4) receives a set of goals. Its mission is to return a list containing those goals that could be validated. Any goal that passes validation is added to the database (after we have made sure that it is not already in there).

```
let backchain(goalset) =                              (5.4)
  { if null(goalset) then nil
    else
      { let x1 = head(goalset)
        let y1 = tail(goalset)
        if valid(x1) and not known(x1) then
            set data = cons(x1,data)
            cons(x1,backchain(y1))
        else
            backchain(y1) } }
```

Validation is carried out by the predicate *valid* (5.5). It first makes sure that there is something to

```
let valid(subgoal) =                                  (5.5)
  { if null(subgoal) then false
    else if known(subgoal) then true
    else if wasasked(subgoal) then false
    else
      { let x = relevant(subgoal,rules)
        if null(x) then ask(subgoal)
        else anyFires(x) } }
```

validate; if not, it returns **false**. Then it looks to
see if the subgoal has already been established and
returns **true** for known items. If it is not known, but
was already asked for, the answer must have been no; so
the return is **false**. If none of these is the case, it
looks to see if there are any relevant rules that it
could use. If it finds no such rule, it asks the user.
If there are relevant rules to try, the return depends
on whether or not one of them can fire.

Let us dispose of the simple predicates *known* and
wasasked: both are tests of membership.

```
let known(g) = member(g,data)
let wasasked(g) = member(g,asked)
```

Finding relevant rules is straightforward: a rule is
relevant to a goal if the goal appears among its
conclusions (5.6).

```
let relevant(g,rrs) =                                    (5.6)
{ if null(rrs) then nil
  else
    { let x = head(rrs)
      let y = tail(rrs)
      if concludes(x,g) then cons(x,relevant(g,y))
      else relevant(g,y) } }
```

Given the selector *consequents* over a rule,
concludes is also a membership test.

```
let concludes(r,g) = member(g,consequents(r))
```

The predicate *anyFires* (5.7) delivers **true** if it
can find one rule that fires. A rule can fire if all
its antecedents are valid.

```
let anyFires(rs) =                                       (5.7)
{ if null(rs) then false
  else if allValid(antecedents(head(rs)) then true
  else anyFires(tail(rs)) }
```

The predicate *allValid* (5.8) delivers **false** if
any of the items fails validation, otherwise it
concludes **true**. To test each item, *allValid* calls
valid. This is how the backward chainer recurses, by
treating antecedents in the same way as it treats top
level goals. Really, the only difference between
backchainer and *allValid* is that the latter needs

to satisfy all its goals in order to succeed, not just one.

```
let allValid(items) =                         (5.8)
{  if null(items) then true
   else if valid(head(items))
       then allValid(tail(items))
   else false }
```

We need one more routine, *ask*(5.9). This presents no problems, as long as we remember to add the item asked for to those already asked and, if the answer is 'yes', to add it also to the database.

```
let ask(item) =                               (5.9)
{  print(item,"?")
   set asked = cons(item,asked)
   if yesp(read) then
       set data = cons(item,data)
       true
   else false }
```

The control routine to set up the environment could be, in its simplest form, something like:

```
set data = nil
set asked = nil
let inferred = backchain(goals)
print("The conclusions are:")
printlist(inferred)
```

We also need to give the rules and the goals.

Example

For our first rule base we shall use a simple example from English grammar, namely the rules for well-formed conditionals. This is not something that presents any difficulties to the native speaker, but is most problematical to those learning English. So our little rule base could, perhaps, form part of some larger system, designed to help students of English.

To use these rules, the student needs to know a few grammatical terms. The sentence that we are aiming to produce is a *conditional* *sentence* or *conditional* which normally comes in the form 'if...then...'. 'If it rains tomorrow, the match will be cancelled' is an example of a conditional sentence. The conditional has two parts, the *condition* ('it rains tomorrow') and the *result* ('the match will be cancelled'). It can describe one of three situations: the relationship between *cause and effect*, a *hypothetical* situation which is either *open* or one that we know to be *contrary to fact or expectation*. The term 'open' is grammatical shorthand for 'not known to be contrary to fact or expectation'. The previous example expresses cause and effect. An example of an open conditional is 'If Anne started her trip last night, she should be in Paris by now'; and one contrary to fact or expectation is 'If Anne had not started her trip last night, she could be coming to the party with us'.

The problems facing the student are numerous: which tense to use for the condition, which construction to use for the result - a simple, tensed verb or an *auxiliary* (like 'shall' or 'can') plus *infinitive* ('to ...') compound - and if the latter, what mood the auxiliary should have - *indicative* ('will') or *subjunctive* ('would') - and what form of infinitive should be used - *ordinary* ('to speak') or *perfect* ('to have spoken').

The rules for a first approximation of the domain that we use to solve this problem are given below. Each rule has three parts: the name of the rule, the antecedent, and the consequent. Both antecedents and consequents can have several parts; if they do, the parts are assumed to be connected by 'and'.

```
rule grammar1
if   conditional describes cause and effect
then use present tense for the condition

rule grammar2
if   conditional describes cause and effect
then use present tense for the result

rule grammar3
if   conditional is hypothetical
     contrary to fact or expectation
then subjunctive

rule grammar4
if   conditional is hypothetical
     open
then indicative
```

```
rule grammar5
if   subjunctive
     condition in the past
then use past perfect for the condition

rule grammar6
if   subjunctive
     condition in the present
then use simple past or present perfect for the condition

rule grammar7
if   subjunctive
     condition in the future
then use simple past or present perfect for the condition

rule grammar8
if   indicative
     condition in the past
then use simple past or present perfect for the condition

rule grammar9
if   indicative
     condition in the present
then use present tense for the condition

rule grammar10
if   indicative
     condition in the future
then use future tense for the condition

rule grammar11
if   subjunctive
then use subjunctive auxiliary for the result

rule grammar12
if   indicative
then use indicative auxiliary for the result

rule grammar13
if   result in the past
then use a perfect infinitive for the result

rule grammar14
if   result in the present
then use an ordinary infinitive for the result
```

```
rule grammar15
if    result in the future
then use an ordinary infinitive for the result
```

And the goals for the system are the various possible forms that parts of the conditional can take:

```
use present tense for the condition
use present tense for the result
use past perfect for the condition
use simple past or present perfect for the condition
use present tense for the condition
use future tense for the condition
use subjunctive auxiliary for the result
use indicative auxiliary for the result
use a perfect infinitive for the result
use an ordinary infinitive for the result
```

A sample run using these goals and rules produced the following dialogue (user inputs are shown in *italics*):

```
Grammatical Advisor

conditional describes cause and effect? n
conditional is hypothetical? y
open? n
contrary to fact or expectation? y
condition in the past? y
condition in the present? n
condition in the future? n
result in the past? n
result in the present? y

My advice is:

use past perfect for the condition
use subjunctive auxiliary for the result
use an ordinary infinitive for the result
```

This may not appear impressive, but nevertheless it is a good beginning. It allows a student to generate a sentence like: 'If Tom had caught the 9 o'clock shuttle, he would be coming up the drive right now.'

But, according to the criteria that we laid down in chapter 3, it is a long way from being a usable expert system. In the next section we explore how we can improve it.

5.4 Improvements

So far we have used only one type of data structure, the list. Although the programs work, restricting ourselves this way leads to unfortunate limitations.

The programs try to establish whether certain items are true or false. Any item that is found to be true is added to the *data* list. This is fine if the item can only have one of two values. But this is not always the case. In our grammatical rule base, the system tries to establish the time of the condition. To do that, it needs to ask three questions - 'condition in the past?', 'condition in the present?', and 'condition in the future?' - store all three as asked and record one of them as true. This is not only irritating to the user, who has every right to complain that he is being asked the *same* question three times, but also illogical and unnecessary.

We can improve the situation by enriching our data structures and using a different method of knowledge representation. Notions such as 'time of the condition', 'time of the result' and 'the situation that the conditional describes' can be easily expressed as object/attribute/value triples. The semantic 'equation' for these triples is:

attribute of *object* = *value*

Using triples, we can overcome the problem of asking the same question several times. We can record in the rule base that the attribute *time* of the object *conditional* can only have one of the values of (*past*, *present*, *future*). Now we need to ask only one question and to record only one answer.

If we arrange that all values are initialised 'unknown', we can also dispense with the list that records which items have already been asked. If an attribute has some value other than 'unknown', we need not ask for it.

We need to elaborate slightly the fundamental scheme of triples. When we talk of an object having attributes, such as an *apple* having a *colour*, we can also talk of attributes of attributes, such as the permissible *range* of colours or the particular *value* for this colour for this apple. To simplify matters, we shall refer to attributes of objects as *parameters* and all other attributes as *attributes*.

Recasting the backward chainer under this scheme of representaion changes it little, but the rules need fundamental revision.

As before, a rule consists of two parts, a list of antecedents and a list of consequents. We shall use the selectors rule.*antecedents* and rule.*consequents* to access these two parts. Whether these are implemented at run-time as functions or whether they are field selectors in the rule base established by a compiler does not alter the algorithms. We can, however, make a note that, as this is static information, it would be more efficient to glean it at compile time. The members of both these lists are *parameter name* and *value* pairs. When applied to the pair *x*, the function *pname(x)* delivers the parameter name, and the function *pvalue(x)* the value.

Example

Our next rule base is a simplified advisor on spots and rashes, perhaps a precursor to a computerised aid for worried parents.

PLEASE NOTE: This rule base was not compiled by a qualified doctor. It would be, therefore, most ill-advised to place any reliance on conclusions drawn from it.

```
rule spots1
if   (appearance weeping/pus-filled_spots)
then (ailment impetigo)

rule spots2
if   (appearance blistery_spots)
     (temperature feverish)
then (ailment chickenpox)

rule spots3
if   (appearance small_pink_spots)
     (temperature feverish)
then (ailment rubella_/german_measles/)
```

```
rule spots4
if   (appearance blotchy_red_areas)
     (temperature feverish)
then (ailment measles)

rule spots5
if   (appearance other)
     (temperature feverish)
then (ailment something_uncommon)

rule spots6
if   (temperature normal)
     (state in_mild_or_no_pain)
     (location feet)
then (ailment athlete's_foot_/tinea/)

rule spots7
if   (temperature normal)
     (state in_severe_pain)
then (ailment shingles)

rule spots8
if   (temperature normal)
     (state in_mild_or_no_pain)
     (location face)
then (ailment acne)

rule spots9
if   (temperature normal)
     (state in_mild_or_no_pain)
     (location where_skin_meets_skin)
then (ailment heat_rash)

rule spots10
if   (temperature normal)
     (state in_mild_or_no_pain)
     (location elsewhere_or_not_localised)
then (ailment something_uncommon)

rule spots11
if   (ailment impetigo)
then (recommendation see_a_doctor_immediately)

rule spots12
if   (ailment chickenpox)
     (state in_severe_pain)
then (recommendation see_a_doctor_immediately)
```

```
rule spots13
if   (ailment rubella_/german_measles/)
     (state in_severe_pain)
then (recommendation see_a_doctor_immediately)

rule spots14
if   (ailment measles)
     (state in_severe_pain)
then (recommendation see_a_doctor_immediately)

rule spots15
if   (ailment something_uncommon)
then (recommendation see_a_doctor_immediately)

rule spots16
if   (ailment shingles)
then (recommendation see_a_doctor_if_it_gets_worse)

rule spots17
if   (ailment athlete's_foot_/tinea/)
then (recommendation see_a_doctor_if_it_gets_worse)

rule spots18
if   (ailment acne)
then (recommendation see_a_doctor_if_it_gets_worse)

rule spots19
if   (ailment heat_rash)
then (recommendation see_a_doctor_if_it_gets_worse)

rule spots20
if   (ailment chickenpox)
     (state in_mild_or_no_pain)
then (recommendation see_a_doctor_if_it_gets_worse)

rule spots21
if   (ailment rubella_/german_measles/)
     (state in_mild_or_no_pain)
then (recommendation see_a_doctor_if_it_gets_worse)

rule spots22
if   (ailment measles)
     (state in_mild_or_no_pain)
then (recommendation see_a_doctor_if_it_gets_worse)
```

Parameters can have several attribute/value pairs.
The most important attribute holds the information

recorded about the parameter; for parameter *p* this can be accessed as *p.value*. Initially these values are set to 'unknown'. The predicate *completed(x)* (5.10) delivers true when *pname(x).value* is no longer 'unknown'.

    let *completed (goal) =*   (5.10)
    { *pname(goal).value ~= 'unknown'* }

The type attribute can be accessed by *p.type*. This can take two values: 'goal' or 'data'. Parameters whose value may be obtained by asking the user are of type 'data'. All other parameters are of type 'goal'. The predicate *askable(x)* delivers **true** for parameters of type 'data'.

The attribute 'display' carries the text associated with the parameter and is accessed with *p.display*. It is used in the dialogue with the user. For example, a little routine that prints a rule in digestible form could be written on the basis of *ruleprint* (5.11). We leave details of the layout to the implementor.

    let *ruleprint(rule) =*   (5.11)
    { *print("if")*
        for each *ip* **in** *rule.antecedents*
            print(pname(ip).display, "is", second(ip))
        print("then")
        for each *tp* **in** *rule.consequents*
            print(pname(tp).display, "is", second(tp)) }

The attribute 'range' gives the list of values that the parameter can take. This a list, and it is used to generate the menu options when asking questions. The attribute 'relevant_rules' has as value a list of those rules that conclude the parameter. For a parameter *p* a rule is relevant if one consequent of the rule is the pair *(p v)* with some value *v*. For a pair *(p v)* a rule is relevant if one consequent is the same pair *(p v)*. We seek relevant rules for two different cases. The first and most obvious case is where we wish to determine a value for a top level goal. In the Spots Advisor this is the 'recommendation'. The second case arises when we are backchaining on the antecedent of a rule and are trying to establish whether the rule can be fired. For example, if the rule under consideration has as one of its antecedents *(temperature feverish)*, we need to access those rules that conclude this. The attribute of 'relevant_rules' could be determined at run-time, but as its information is static, that is, it does not change during the course of consultation, it is more efficient to calculate it beforehand, during compilation.

The pre-defined parameters, in the absence of a compiler, have to be specifically given. For the Spots Advisor they are as follow (with the exception of *relevant_rules*)

```
goals = (recommendation)

ailment.rank = goal
ailment.value = unknown
ailment.display =
   "what_the_patient_is_likely_to_bbe_suffering_from"

recommendation.rank = goal
recommendation.value = unknown
recommendation.display = "the_recommendation"

temperature.rank = data
temperature.value = unknown
temperature.display =
   "the_temperature_of_the_patient"
temperature.range = (normal feverish)

appearance.rank = data
appearance.value = unknown
appearance.display = "the_appearance_of_the_rash"
appearance.range = (blistery_spots small_pink_spots
   blotchy_red_areas weeping/pus-filled_spots)

state.rank = data
state.value = unknown
state.display = "the_state_of_the_patient"
state.range = (in_severe_pain in_mild_or_no_pain)

location.rank = data
location.value = unknown
location.display = "the_location_of_the_rash"
location.range = (face feet where_skin_meets_skin
   elsewhere_or_not_localised)

objects = (ailment recommendation temperature
   state appearance location)
```

The role of the *backchain* (5.12) is very much reduced to keeping track of the goals. The reason for this is to make amendments easier. This version tries all goals. It is a simple matter to modify it so that it stops on the first successfully established goal.

```
let backchain (goalset) =                          (5.12)
{ for each goal in goalset
    if not completed(goal) then trygoal(goal) }
```

Strictly speaking, the test before *trygoal* is not necessary as *trygoal* will test that the goal is not already completed, but it provides a measure of improvement. The function *trygoal(goal)* is again much the same. If the goal is not already completed, it looks for a relevant rule and tests if the rule can fire. If all the rule's antecedents are valid, all its consequents are concluded. If it cannot succeed with a rule, it asks the user.

The job of *trygoal* (5.13) is to go through the rules relevant to the goal until it finds one that can fire. If it runs out of relevant rules without completing the goal, and if the goal is askable, it asks the user. If the goal is not askable, *trygoal* does nothing. It is not immediately obvious that this gives the desired behaviour, so let us look at a

```
let trygoal(goal) =                                (5.13)
{ for each rule in goal.relevant_rules
      until completed(goal)
    { if allvalid(rule.antecedents)
      then fire(rule.consequents)
    if askable(pname(goal)) and not completed(goal)
    then answer(goal) }
```

concrete example. In trying to establish the top goal ('recommendation'), the first hypothesis (the subgoal 'ailment') is that the patient is suffering from impetigo. If the symptoms are not those of impetigo, we do not want the system to ask about 'ailment'; we want it to abandon the hypothesis, that is the rule that concludes a recommendation if the ailment is impetigo, and try a different one. Opinions differ on what should happen if there are no further hypotheses to try. Some systems, when they run out of rules to try, will ask the user. Some would argue that this is wrong for the following reason: a goal, whether it is top level or not, is a representation of the problem that the user brings to the system; the system should not turn around and ask the user to solve his problem. The Spots Advisor should produce a recommendation irrespective of whether it can identify the ailment or not. Another application could legitimately say to the user 'I cannot help you, I have not got enough information.'

Validating a rule (5.14) is modified somewhat. There are now additional possibilities to take care of. An antecedent may be known but, unlike the previous version, it may have the wrong value. If the value for the antecedent is not known, *allvalid* recurses, but, again, it needs to test that it has the right value.

```
let allvalid(antes) =                              (5.14)
  { if null(antes) then true
    else if valid(head(antes))
        then allvalid(tail(antes))
    else if completed(head(antes)) then false
    else
      { backchain(head(antes))
        if valid(head(antes))
            then allvalid(tail(antes))
        else false } }
```

An item is an attribute/value pair. To test that it is valid, we need to compare that the value of the pair is the value recorded in the database against the attribute. This is the job of *valid* (5.15).

```
let valid(ante) =                                  (5.15)
  { pname(ante).value = second(ante) }
```

Firing a rule (5.16) consists of recording the value against each attribute found in the consequents of the rule.

```
let fire(conseqs) =                                (5.16)
  { for each c in conseqs
    set pname(c).value = second(c) }
```

Asking the user about an item (5.17) is now a bit more complex. Instead of asking him for a simple 'yes or no', we present him with a multiple choice question.

The text of the question we get from the attribute 'display', and the text for the choices from 'range'.

```
let answer(goal) =                              (5.17)
{   print("What is the", pname(goal).display, "?")
    set pname(goal).value =
            choose(pname(goal).range) }

let choose(options) =
{   show(options, 1, length(options))
    loop
        print("Your choice:")
        let ans = read()
        if ans = "why" then justify()
    until 0 < ans <= length(options)
    pick(ans, options) }

let show(list, lo, hi) =
{   print("[", lo, "]", pick(lo, list))
    show(list, lo+1, hi) }
```

The routine *show* assumes that 0 < hi and lo <= hi. The *length* of the options list can be calculated simply at run time, or can be set at compile time. We do not give the text of the function. The function *pick(n, list)* delivers the n'th member of the list.

The main control is

```
for each ob in objects
    set ob.value = 'unknown'
backchain(goals)
print("The results of the consultation are:")
for each ob in objects
    if ob.type = 'goal'
    then print(ob.display, ob.value)
```

Here is a sample session with the Spots Advisor (user input is shown again in *italics*):

```
What is the the appearance of the rash?
    [ 1 ] blistery spots
    [ 2 ] small pink spots
    [ 3 ] blotchy red areas
    [ 4 ] weeping/pus-filled spots
    Your choice: 2
```

What is the the temperature of the patient?
    [1] normal
    [2] feverish
    Your choice: *1*

What is the the state of the patient?
    [1] in severe pain
    [2] in mild or no pain
    Your choice: *2*

What is the the location of the rash?
    [1] face
    [2] feet
    [3] where skin meets skin
    [4] elsewhere or not localised
    Your choice: *3*

The results of the consultation are:

The patient is likely to be suffering from heat rash
The recommendation is see a doctor if it gets worse·

5.5 Summary

Our aim in this chapter was to examine how an expert
system operates. To achieve this aim, we implemented a
forward chainer and a backward chainer, the latter in
two variants using different data structures. On the
basis of these implementations we can draw a number of
conclusions. The most important of these is the claim
that we set out with: the algorithms underlying expert
systems are neither unusual nor inherently difficult.
There is nothing in these algorithms that someone with
a reasonable understanding of data structures and a
firm grasp of production systems could not reproduce
once shown how to start. This is, hopefully, what this
chapter has done. We must not forget, however, that
this simplicity was achieved only after many false
starts and the elimination of many blind alleys by
those who have gone before us. Neither should we think
that we are now at the end of the road. Just as the
first backward chainer could be improved, so can the
second. Although the data structures used give it
reasonable power and expressiveness, they are still not
enough. They provide the means to record attribute
values for objects, but not the means to handle

multiple objects. For example, it would be difficult to keep track of the four wheels on a car in a fault diagnosis system or the variable number of children in different families that a social security advisor system would need. However, these deficiencies can be repaired by introducing further, more powerful data structures and adjusting the backward chainer to handle them. But elaborations of this kind are software engineering - not Artificial Intelligence - tasks.

Further reading

P.H. Winston and B.K.P. Horn describe a rule handler in their book *LISP* (Addison-Wesley, 1981).

For a thorough discussion of semantic triples - their philosophical, psychological, computational, and linguistic aspects - read J.F. Sowa's *Conceptual Structures: Information Processing in Mind and Machine* (Addison-Wesley, 1984). If you plan to develop expert systems seriously, this book should give you a sound intellectual base to build on, although it is not for the faint-hearted.

The method of using accumulating parameters - as used, for example, in the forward chainer - is described in Peter Henderson's *Functional Programming: Application and Implementation* (Prentice-Hall, 1980).

6 Validation

6.1 Why validate?

Having got a working skeletal expert system and some
rules for our application, we are faced with the
inevitable question: does it work? This, again, is a
question that expert systems pose in common with
conventional computer systems. In just the same way
that conventional applications need to be validated, so
does ours. In fact, the need for validation is even
greater. Conventional applications start on much firmer
ground; the algorithms that they implement rest on
scientific laws, established professional or business
practices, or equally well-assured grounds. In
contrast, what we are implementing is far less assured,
resting mainly on heuristics, rules of thumb or, at
most, formulations borne out by practice but never
subjected to rigorous examination before.

There is also a second, but equally important
reason. Conventional applications tend to be used in
such a way that, whenever they malfunction, it is
relatively easy to detect that they are misbehaving.
There are exceptions, of course; large, complex systems
can fail in subtle and unexpected ways. Nevertheless,
the point stands: even complex systems, when they
misbehave, produce effects that we can label as wrong.
The case is not so clear-cut when we come to expert
systems. Sir Geoffrey Vickers in *The Art of Judgement:
A Study in Policy Making* (1968) states that the only
way to assess the correctness of judgements is by the
exercise of the same faculty. The point he makes is
that we cannot establish the correctness of judgements
by results alone. A particular judgement may have been
'correct' at the time it was reached, even if its
consequences turned out to be undesirable.

Sir Geoffrey's claim points not only to the greater need for validation but also to its difficulties. The problem is this: when can we pronounce a judgemental system to be correct? When the MYCIN team embarked on their validation programme - and MYCIN is probably the best and most exhaustively tested expert system - they ran up against precisely this problem. In their first attempt at validation they were comparing MYCIN's conclusions against what actually was the case, that is, against reality. They found, however, that the system's performance was very poor when judged by this criterion. The question that they had to ask was whether it is justifiable to judge its performance against actuality. Is it reasonable to expect MYCIN to perform better than leading experts in the field? Or should we judge its effectiveness against the performance of experts? Later trials compared its performance against that of specialists in the field and also against that of medically trained people who were not, however, specialists in the field of blood infection and bacterial meningitis. MYCIN performed better than the specialists and much better than the non-specialists.

Is this a justifiable procedure? The debate has barely begun, and it will be a long time before it reaches some sort of concensus of opinion. The outcome very much depends on the way that we intend to use expert systems. There are two extremes to the spectrum of usage. At one end we find systems being looked upon and used as replacements for an expert, their findings and recommendations being treated in the same way as we would the pronouncements of a live expert. At the other end we find the view that these systems are no more than very convenient-to-use books, which retrieve information only if relevant to the problem at hand. The chief difference between these two views is how much the user of such a system surrenders his judgement and accountability to the system and how much of it he retains.

Most systems probably lie somewhere between these two extremes. But the position of each has to be carefully assessed, because it dictates what passes for a reasonable procedure for validation. The greater the degree of surrender, the greater is the need for *objective* verification; for if we follow advice from these systems heedlessly, we care not whether their judgement was 'fine' or 'misguided'; we are interested only in the results. In my view, a total suspension of our critical faculties is not only irrational but also extremely dangerous. It tacitly relies on machines performing in matters of judgement better than humans. If the best brains in the world cannot get the economy right, where is the knowledge going to come from for a machine to do better? And even if the knowledge of the system is gleaned from a scientifically strong discipline, it has to be totally judgement-free before we can rely on it with complete assurance.

Wherever our system sits on this scale, the requirement for validation stands. The only variations that we are allowed are in its stringency and severity.

6.2 What to validate?

Given the imperative to validate, the next question that we must ask is just what do we validate for, and what should our validation procedures be?

We look upon an expert system as valid if its pronouncements are free from contradiction, if it can tackle any problem within its domain, if it can deliver the right answers, if the strength of its conviction is commensurate with the data and the knowledge at hand, and if it can be used with reasonable facility by those for whom it was designed. Thus, there are five basic requirements:

1. consistency
2. completeness
3. soundness
4. precision and
5. usability.

We shall analyse each of these requirements in turn and attempt to identify ways of testing for them. Unfortunately, the technology of expert systems is not sufficiently well established as yet to give us reliable and ready-to-use tools for every occasion; so in some areas we have to make do with less than perfect means.

6.2.1 Consistency

The requirement for consistency demands that the system should produce similar answers to similar questions. Indeed, it is often put forward as one of the greatest benefits we can derive from using expert systems, namely that their answers do not vary according to extraneous circumstances like the day of the week or how tired we feel.

Given any requirement, we need to examine two questions: is it reasonable and, if it is, how do we attain it?

The consistency requirement is eminently reasonable: an inconsistent system would be unusable. Even with human experts, who do suffer from fatigue and oversight occasionally, while we allow them inconsistencies in minor matters, we expect them to act consistently on major ones. From a machine, as it is not subject to the same limitations, we expect no such discrepancies.

How can we validate a system for consistency? The first thing to note is that there are no general methods for proving this. There are, however, tests that we can perform which, although they do not furnish us with a proof, can increase our confidence. Some of these tests are very simple to perform. We have already met one in conjunction with what the compiler could do for us. This is a formal test designed to ensure that no two rules come to opposing conclusions from the same premises. But passing this test is by itself no guarantee of consistency - at least not for our purposes - for it does not prove that *similar* cases will be treated similarly. When an expert recommends a particular course of action, we expect him not to invert his judgement if we alter the situation in some minor aspect. Unfortunately, until we can produce a rigorous notion of similarity and can apply it to these systems, we shall have no tool, no algorithm for proving consistency. But we can at least run some tests to uncover possible inconsistencies.

What are the manifestations of inconsistency? In chapter 4 we saw an example in which both a conclusion and its denial were obtained from the same data. We can generalise this from a dichotomy - an 'A or non-A' situation - to the case where the answer space is divided into more than two parts. We can enlarge it, for example, from a system that concludes that 'the patient should/should not take aspirin' to one that advises on a number of different drugs. This, in fact, is the more usual situation. Systems that classify, diagnose or advise, all have to select from a set of possibilities, where the set has more than two members. How do we judge the consistency in such cases? There are three possibilities.

In the first case, the set of answers is divided into collectively exhaustive but mutually exclusive, classes. A very simple example would be classifying investors according to the tax bracket that they fall into. In such a case, inconsistency is easy to recognise - though it may not be easy to find.

The second, and more usual, possibility is that, although the classes are collectively exhaustive, they are not mutually exclusive. Any classification that admits borderline cases falls into this category. But even with these we can usualy tell an inconsistency when we see one. Borderline cases usually border on two possibilities. 'Spots and fever indicate measles or rubella but definitely not laryngitis.' So if the rules can nevertheless deduce laryngitis, we can judge them to be inconsistent. (Note that this is a static test on the rule base: we are looking for rules that *can* deduce non-overlapping cases, not rules that *will* deduce them.)

There is also a third, but mercifully rare, case in which all the classes overlap. How many strands of hair must a man have to stop being bald? Can we justifiably call a set of rules inconsistent if, on the basis of area of head covered, it pronounces him to be bald but, on the basis of number of hairs, it does not?

The pre-condition to this test is straightforward but, in the case of expert systems, often forgotten. We must specify what distinctions matter to us; given such a specification we can then say, should our set of rules simultaneously opt for both sides of a distinction, that such rules are inconsistent. The test, unfortunately, is capable only of finding inconsistencies and not of proving consistency.

This test is easier to perform if we can apply a graph traverser to our rule set and, through its use, establish what paths exist between input data and conclusions.

6.2.2 Completeness

We can talk of completeness in two separate senses. One we have already encountered in chapter 3. In the sense used there, completeness describes a total coverage of the domain - or specified part of the domain - by the knowledge base. Whenever such completeness can be obtained, everything derivable in the domain from the given data will be derived. We could refer to this sense as *semantic* completeness. In contrast, the second sense refers to *formal* completeness. It concentrates purely on the form rather than on the content of the knowledge base. This is the sense we shall use in this chapter.

The purely practical - rather than some theoretical - requirement of completeness demands that our knowledge base is sufficiently wide in its coverage to allow the system to tackle successfully any problem within its domain. Again, we ask the same two questions as before.

Is this requirement reasonable? Perhaps surprisingly, the answer depends on circumstances. If we are dealing with a problem space that can be partitioned into a practically enumerable set of equivalence classes, the requirement is very reasonable. When we are provided with a set of rules to advise us on how to play a King-and-Pawn *versus* King-and-Quueen endgame - here the number of possible positions is finite and enumerable - we would have every cause to complain if the rules could not handle some of these positions. Another example is the case of company rules covering allowable expense claims. Again, the classes of claims are finite, and we would be in a quandary (and so would the accounts department) if some classes were not covered. But, let us take the example of a financial advisory system. The classes of clients that it can handle is finite, but the number of the different recommendations it could make on when to invest, how much, and in what securities is so large that it would take an unreasonable time to enumerate. In this case we would not be much upset if some combinations were never considered by the system. The notion of reasonable enumerability may not be very clear and precise mathematically, but it is crystal clear to the practical man.

Completeness without any bounds or constraints is an intractable idea. Even mathematicians talk of completeness only under the assumption of a closed world in which, for example, every statement must be either true or false. The demand for completeness in such a world is the demand that everything that is true is derivable by the (mathematical) system. And to those who dislike mathematical or philosophical arguments we can put the following question about the financial advisor: What proof would convince you that this system considers all possible investment combinations?

Completeness matters only in the face of the countable. The practical person's answer to the last question would be that he does not much care whether the system is combinatorially complete in its *detailed* advice, but cares very much that is should consider all possible *classes* of investment.

When we adopt the practical outlook, we also have a clear idea of just what sort of completeness we need to prove. We can ask questions, examine knowledge bases, and satisfy ourselves that the system caters for everything that is material to the purpose of our system and that we can enumerate. We can list the classes of investment that we are concerned with - securities, annuities, mortgages, saving schemes, etc. - and make sure that there are rules concluding each. We can list the classes of investors that we cater for - by their age, by their earning power, by the term of their investment, by their debts and commitments, etc. - and make sure there are rules that take these factors as their antecedents. We can probe the warp and weft of our rule base along each countable dimension for completeness. Indeed, if we can list all classes of conclusion and all classes of input data, we can automate the test: the compiler can check that all inputs appear as antecedents, all outputs as consequents, and that there is at least one path from the inputs to the outputs. Even if tests like these do not guarantee theoretical completeness, we should do at least this much in order to uncover obvious gaps or disjointedness in the rule set.

We have already met the need for specifying the distinctions that we expect the system to draw. The need for clear specifications of what the system is expected to do is even more important when it comes to assessing completeness. The specifications for an investment advisor should state clearly what classes of investment will be considered and what classes will not. Will it consider and evaluate financial options such as local authority loans, second mortgages, emigrating to a tax-haven, voluntary liquidation, option dealing, and so on? Given such a specification, we can start on a completeness check along the following lines:

1. First we check that all specified outcomes ('top goals') can be produced by our rules.
2. We can then check that the antecedents to these goals are sufficient to differentiate them. We

ask questions like: In a system that tries to make sense of sonar returns, can we distinguish a submarine from a whale, a wreck, a sea pinnacle, a ship, or a shoal of fish?

Analysis, along lines like this, will uncover our information requirements. Some of this information we can obtain directly from the input; other parts will constitute lower level goals. These intermediate goals need to be treated just like the top level goals and be analysed for completeness. But performing analysis at this level suffers from the added difficulty that we can no longer rely on our specifications to indicate gaps. If we have established in our sonar data analysis system - for the sake of argument - distance, velocity and sound produced as intermediate goals, the specification will not tell us that we also need size as a goal. We need to seek help from the domain specialist to spot gaps like these.

3. If we repeatedly perform this step, we arrive eventually at the bottom, at the data level. We can now reverse the process and work from the data towards the conclusions. What we should check for on this pass is that all possible values in the data are used by the rules. If our rules deal only with signal strengths below 1 dB and above 5 dB, we have a gap. Filling these gaps is very likely to demand new rules which, in turn, will generate new intermediate or even top level goals.

Working this way repeatedly - first backwards from the goal to the data, then from the data towards the goals - will give us the opportunity to provide support for unsupported goals and to make use of or discard unused data and intermediate goals.

6.2.3 Soundness

To the mathematician, soundness is the converse of completeness. Whereas completeness demands that everything true is derivable, soundness demands that everything derivable is true. In the context of expert systems, soundness means that the system comes to the right conclusions, where 'right' means - in light of the points already raised - 'in agreement with expert judgement'.

From a practical point of view, this requirement is, again, obviously reasonable: an unsound system is useless.

What we need to do is also clear, although this does not render it easy to do. A moment's reflection will show that to *prove* soundness is not practicable: we would need to show agreement between the expert and the system in every conceivable case. We can, and should, however, *test* for soundness. A workable test procedure is to obtain, either from our expert or from the archives, a set of testcases and a recommended or expected conclusion for each - in precisely the same way as we test conventional systems.

6.2.4 Precision

The requirement of precision is specific to systems that deliver probabilistic or qualified judgements. Soundness demands that the system comes to the right conclusion, precision that it presents this conclusion with a certainty appropriate to the case. It is an extension of the requirement for soundness.

Our reason for the requirement stems from a desire not to be confronted with a system given to bouts of over-confidence or pessimism, and especially not in an unpredictable mix. We can compensate for a consistently optimistic or consistently pessimistic system, but we cannot use one that unpredictably swings from one to the other.

How do we test for precision? The first decision that we have to make is what bounds can we accept on the answers or, in other words, how inaccurate can the answer be and still remain acceptable? Unfortunately, there can be no general answer, for what constitutes acceptable precision is application-dependent. But can we not at least say something about the acceptable limits on probabilistic answers? Surely, some errors are always unacceptable, like reporting +0.8 instead of -0.8, or even reporting 0.8 instead of 0.3. But is 0.8 instead of 0.6 classifiable as an error? The answer is that 'it depends'. One could argue, as some do, that subjectively we differentiate only a few cases: certainty, strong evidence, weak evidence, and uncertainty. Given such limited differentiation as the above categories, we need satisfy ourselves only that the system is accurate within these broad ranges. But the difficulty remains; we cannot say, in general, where the divisions should be placed or even whether these ranges are sufficiently accurate for our particular application. The practical answer remains the same: accuracy is domain-dependent. We need to define what accuracy we want and make sure that we get it.

To improve the precision of a rule base, one of the most powerful methods available to the knowledge engineer is sensitivity analysis. What this method establishes is the variability in the conclusions as a function of the variability of data; or to put it more simply, what difference will it make to the conclusion if we answer one of the questions differently. If the conclusion remains the same, the question is not sensitive; if, however, small deviations in the answer lead to large differences in the conclusion, the question is said to be very sensitive. Good expert systems shells provide some means of automating this analysis. One very effective method of automating it is to display as a histogram output values against possible answers of one input - the question whose sensitivity we are investigating - as the independent variable.

The object of the exercise is to locate sensitive spots in the model. A sensitive spot is one that produces large changes in the output against small changes in the input. When histogramming is available, sensitive points can be easily identified because the output graph shows one or more sharp transitions (discontinuities, in mathematical terminology). In general, models tend to have few sensitive points; answers to most questions and deductions from most intermediate goals produce smooth transitions in the output. Sensitivity analysis, although it takes some time to do, saves a lot of effort in the end, for it allows the knowledge engineer to concentrate his efforts on getting accurate values for only those parameters that will have a major influence on the outcome.

6.2.5 Usability

In expert systems there is far more opportunity than in other systems to introduce ambiguities in the questions put to the user and a greater risk for the user to misunderstand what is asked of him, to answer the wrong question, or to answer the right one but incorrectly. The reason for this is that we use prose rather than codification to communicate with him. A natural language interface has often been seen as highly desirable and something that we should aim for. Now that we have taken a few faltering footsteps towards such an interface and welcome its advantages with open arms, its disadvantages also become very apparent. Natural language is inherently ambiguous, and this ambiguity manifests itself at every opportunity in the question and answer sessions of a consultation. If there is a way to misunderstand or misconstrue a question the system puts, somebody, some time will do just that.

When we talk of the usability requirement, what we mean is not what the fashionable but loose term 'user friendliness' aims at. We mean, simply, that the interaction between the user and the system should proceed as intended by the designer. There are several considerations at issue here, which can be best described, perhaps, by way of some examples.

'How certain are you that the colour of the sparking plug is grey (-5..+5)?'

(The -5..+5 indicates that we should answer in that range, with +5 meaning absolute certainty, -5 absolute certainty that whatever is asked is *not* the case, 0 showing absence of information; and usually we are allowed to pick any number in that range, like 2.35.)

Taken literally, we can answer this question only with +5 or -5; there is no doubt about whichever is the case, the plug being grey or not being grey. But, perhaps, what the question tries to elicit is how grey or how near to grey is the plug. How do we answer, then, if the plug is brown? It would be better to ask

'What is the colour of the sparking plug:
    [1] white
    [2] grey
    [3] brown
    [4] black?'

followed perhaps by

    'What is its state:
      [1] dry
      [2] oily?'

'How certain are you that x (-5..+5)?' is a canned phrase that appears often in expert systems. Although we can sympathise with the designer - he wants to establish a probability, however subjective - the phrase is most unfortunate. It commits the fallacy of many questions (just like 'have you stopped beating your wife'). Specifically, it asks two questions:

1. What is the probability of x being the case?
2. What is your conviction of x being the case?

These two questions are independent. The difficulty facing the responder is which question to answer. And he must opt for one or the other. The difficulty of the designer is that he will not know which option the user will pick.

    'How likely is it that the shuttle will not leave
    on time (-5..+5)?'

This question poses several difficulties as well. Its first and most severe shortcoming is that it forces a mental somersault. "I am certain that the shuttle will not leave on time; 'certain that not...' is shown by -5. But the question asks '...will *not* leave on time...'. So do I have to invert the answer to +5?"
    All negative questions suffer from this. A better formulation would be "...that the shuttle will be delayed..." and the inversion is done by the rule.
    Its second shortcoming is that it gives no guidance on degree. How do we answer if the flight is definitely going to be late but only by one minute? Definitely 'not on time' requires +5. But a difference of one minute would swing the answer to -5 ("certain that 'not on time' is not the case"). A swing from one end of the scale to the other for a one minute difference seems excessive. Perhaps the answer for only a little bit late should be a little bit less than +5, say +4.5. And now we have to choose between -5 and +4.5! What reliance can the system place on our answer?
    Again, a menu type question will get us out of a lot of difficulties, something along the lines of

'The shuttle will be most likely:
```
[ 1 ] on time
[ 2 ] up to 10 minutes late
[ 3 ] up to an hour late
[ 4 ] cancelled?'
```

or whatever intervals are the most suitable.

Then there are questions not with an ambiguous scale, but with the wrong one, like

'How frequently do you suffer from insomnia (-5..+5)?'

This is silly. A better form is again a menu:

'How frequently do you suffer from insomnia:
```
[ 1 ] every night
[ 2 ] once a week
[ 3 ] once a month
[ 4 ] rarely
[ 5 ] never?'
```

Of course, if our system allows only -5..+5 type questions, we have a problem. But even then we can do better with

'How often do you suffer from insomnia (-5 = never, 0 = once a month, +5 = permanently) (-5..+5)?'

Finally, let us look at an example that appears wrong, but is not:

'What is you salary (range 1..1000)?'

A number of difficulties and questions confront the user when trying to answer this question:

1. What does he mean by salary? Gross or net? Including bonus and overtime payments or not?
2. Working for the Dutch office, I get paid in guilders. Should I give the answer in guilders or in pounds sterling?
3. Is he asking for weekly, monthly, or yearly salary?

It would be a mistake to cram all these details in the question. Their appearance would be very helpful on the first occasion that we use the system, a growing source of irritation as we get used to it, and an intolerable verbosity once we become experienced users. The correct place for the detail is in the help text. Most commercially produced expert system shells allow us to specify such text, some at more than one level. It gets displayed at the user's request, that is only when he needs it. In this way we can avoid rendering the system pedestrian and verbose - the sins of many 'user friendly' systems.

Even if we take all precautions to make sure that the user interface is clean and unambiguous, we still need to carry out tests of usability.

One such test probes repeatability. This is a test that designers of survey questionnaires are very familiar with and use often. It is performed by asking a group of users to present a particular case to the system - the case does not need to be the same across users. Their answers to the questions put by the system are recorded and compared with a repetition of the test, say, a week later. To pass the test, there must be no significant deviation between the first and second sets of answers. Of course, what constitutes a significant deviation is domain-dependent.

Another test is less formal and less rigorous, but can be just as informative. Before releasing the system, a representative group of users is first of all given whatever training all users are intended to receive. They are then asked to use the system in the presence of an observer. The point of the test is to highlight what difficulties the users encounter. They are allowed, even encouraged, to ask questions and to report their comments. These must be recorded and analysed after the test. These records are a goldmine of information not only on ambiguities in the system but also on how to improve the wording of questions, help text, and presentation of results. The ideal, probably never attained, is that the user sails through the session, never gets stuck, never hesitates, and always gives the correct answer.

Further reading

The nature, process, and verifiability of judgements is laid bare in the book by Sir Geoffrey Vickers, *The Art of Judgement: A Study in Policy Making* (University Paperbacks, Methuen, 1968) and should be made compulsory reading for prospective knowledge engineers.

7 Facilities

In chapter 5 we created a basic expert system shell. This shell lacks some important facilities that were outlined in chapter 3 and classed as desirable. In this chapter we examine some of the missing facilities, in particular those of explanation, justification and provision for handling uncertainty. But first we identify a simple, but nevertheless important extension.

7.1 Questions

The shell, as it stands, can ask only multiple choice questions. Restricting ourselves to this would be just as limiting as having to cast every question in the 'How certain are you that...' mould. Fortunately, the mechanism used can be easily extended to cater for other types.

In practice, the following question types have been found to be the most useful in addition to multiple choice:

1. Yes/No: although this could be implemented using the multiple choice mechanism, users prefer to answer with 'Y' or 'N', rather than '1' or '2'. It is good practice, anyway, not to force the user to encode his answers if it can be avoided. The question should be marked as a Yes/No question.
2. Free answer: any answer is accepted. This is useful for getting such details as the client's name, address, occupation, etc.
3. Number: this expects a numeric answer within a certain range. The range should be indicated in the question.

7.2 Explanations

The next facility that we tackle is explanation. The question that we must ask first of all is this: When the user asks for an explanation, what does he expect to get? This is a question that has interested and exercised philosophers for quite some time. It is useful, therefore, to see what they have to say on the subject.

According to Robert H. Ennis in his *Logic in Teaching* (1969) there are two items in every explanation:

1. the *explicandum*, the thing to be explained, and
2. the *explicans*, the material offered as explanatory.

And there are three kinds of explanation:

1. interpretive
2. descriptive
3. reason giving

Interpretive explanation gives and clarifies the meaning of terms. In this sense, definition is a form of interpretive explanation. It may be called *explaining what*. Chapter 3 has two very good examples of interpretive explanation: the reported usage by practitioners of the term *knowledge* and the working definition of *expert system*.

Descriptive explanation describes a process or a structure. It does so by stating facts, relations, criteria, purposes, steps, parts, etc. It may be termed *explaining how*. Explaining how the car works, how an inference engine works, how to make ice-cream, how to submit a job to the batch queue, or the structure of parliament are all examples of descriptive explanation.

Reason-giving explanation, as its name implies, explains by stating reasons, causes, laws, and the like. In such an explanation we are seeking some fact or claim from which the thing to be explained logically follows. It could be termed *explaining why*. Giving the causes of the French Revolution or why the fuse blew are examples of reason-giving explanation.

The user of an expert system could require any of the three types of explanation. Although many systems provide a lot of good explanatory facilities, no system can provide, as yet, explanations as good as those that we can expect from experts. There are several reasons for this. First of all an expert system does not tailor its explanations to the inquirer, whereas an expert would take into account the knowledge and background of the inquirer and adjust his explanations accordingly. Secondly, an important part of the process of explanation is the feedback that the expert gets from his client which allows him to detect particular points of difficulty and to divert the course of the explanation accordingly. Lastly, the logical connection between *explicans* and *explicandum* is often logically less than strict; some clients would see this connection and grasp its sufficiency immediately, some would get the point later, others perhaps never. Unless we are dealing with a field in some strict scientific discipline, explanations will remain an individual affair. Those methods that we do have at our disposal do not give us the power to handle such a wide spectrum. What we can provide is often less than ideal, but still very much needed.

Most expert systems provide explanatory facilities of all three kinds.

7.2.1 Elaboration

When the user of an expert system is asked a question, the terms used in the question may be unknown to him or may appear ambiguous to him. The system could and should provide some help. This is usually achieved by providing some elaboration text to accompany the question. Some systems provide such text at several levels, each successive level giving more and more detailed explanations of the terms used in the question, of the underlying assumptions, of the background assumed by the question, or any other material which may help the user to answer the question that the designer wanted him to answer. These all come under the heading of *interpretive explanations* or *explaining what*. They also go by the name of *elaborations*.

We have come across a particular use for this sort of explanation in section 6.2.5 in the 'What is your salary?' example. Employing our scheme of attribute-value pairs, we can add this facility very easily. We need to provide three things. First, some

way for the user to signal that he needs help with the
question. Typing a '?' instead of the answer is a good
way. (Typing 'help' is usually reserved for providing
information and guidance on how to use the system and
its facilities.) Secondly, the routine that asks
questions of the user must look out for this and, if
found, retrieve the help text one by one (finishing
off, perhaps, with a 'Sorry, no further help is
available'). And lastly, we must provide the help text.
The easiest way is to create further attribute/value
pairs. For our example it could be:

```
salary.display = "What is your salary"
salary.help1 = "The question asks for your monthly
      salary to the nearest 10 pounds sterling."
salary.help2 = "The amount asked for is your gross
      income, that is before tax and other deductions,
      but excluding bonus, overtime or commission."
```

7.2.2 Justification

We have already discussed the need for *explaining why*
in chapter 3. Often the user wants to know why he is
being asked a question. The simple explanation is that
his answer will help the system to try to solve his
problem. This, however, he knows already, and what he
expects to receive is the detailed way in which his
answer would contribute to solving the problem. What a
backward chainer is trying to do is to verify one of
its goals; that is why it needs the answer, directly or
indirectly. What it can give, therefore, to the user by
way of explanation is the implicative chain that leads
from his answer to the goal hypothesis under
consideration. Indeed, many systems do just that, and
most users find this adequate. It is a particular form
of *reason-giving* explanation that is more commonly
known as *justification*.

Again, we need to take care of three things. The
first is to receive requests for justification from the
user. As the user is going to ask for this only when he
is being asked a question, the best place to capture
his request is in the *choose* procedure. The way that
it is implemented here, when this facility is required,
is that the user types 'why' instead of his answer.
The modified procedure is given in (7.1).

```
let choose(options) =                              (7.1)
  { show(options, 1, length(options))
    loop
        print("Your choice:")
        let ans = read()
        if ans = "why" then justify()
    until 0 < ans <= length(options)
    pick(ans, options) }
```

The second item on our agenda is to ensure that we have all the information that we need to service the request. Different systems provide different variants of justification. Some will display the entire chain between the goal and the question, others will display only parts. In the latter case usually the user is allowed to specify how far back the chain should be displayed. The implementation here belongs to the first variety.

If our system follows the standard method of implementing procedures in high-level languages, namely by the use of run-time stacks, the necessary information will already be there: on one of the stacks. But unless we are willing to - or even allowed to - access it by some tricky programming, we cannot make use of it. So we need to create our own data structure to hold the current consultation path from the top goal to the question asked. What this needs to hold is the sequence of rules that the system is trying to fire. As the data structure is a stack, we need to define the usual *push* and *pop* operations. We also need to initialise the stack. We assume that these have been done. The obvious place for capturing and releasing the rules under consideration is in *trygoal* (7.2).

```
let trygoal(goal) =                                (7.2)
  { for each rule in goal.relevant_rules
        until completed(goal)
      { push(rule)
        if allvalid(rule.antecedents)
        then fire(rule.consequents)
        pop(rule) }
    if askable(first(goal)) and not completed(goal)
    then answer(goal) }
```

Our third task is to display the justification itself when requested. This routine works its way back,

taking rules off the stack. Each rule it displays is in
three parts:

1. Those antecedents in the condition part that are
   completed. These represent information that the
   system already knows.
2. The remainder of the antecedents - including the
   one relating to the question. These represent
   information that the system hopes to gain.
3. The consequents which, if the antecedents in part
   two can be completed, will be concluded.

Only the bare bones of the routine are given here
(7.3). The details are, to some   extent,   a   matter   of
taste. The sample session gives one set of choices.

```
let justify() =                                    (7.3)
    for each r in stack
        for each completed(a) in antecedents(r)
            print_known(a)
        for each not completed(a) in antecedents(r)
            print_not_yet_known(a)
        for each c in consequents(r)
            print_deducible(c)
```

A sample session with Spots Advisor showing the use
of the justification facility produced the following
run-time listing (user inputs are given in *italics*):

```
What is the the appearance of the rash?
    [ 1 ] blistery spots
    [ 2 ] small pink spots
    [ 3 ] blotchy red areas
    [ 4 ] weeping/pus-filled spots
    Your choice: 2

What is the the temperature of the patient?
    [ 1 ] normal
    [ 2 ] feverish
    Your choice: why

I already know that
    the appearance of the rash is small pink spots
so that if
    the temperature of the patient is feverish
then
    what the patient is likely to be suffering from
        is rubella /german measles/
```

and if
    what the patient is likely to be suffering from
        is rubella /german measles/
and if
    the state of the patient is in severe pain
then
    the recommendation is see a doctor immediately

    Your choice: *2*

What is the the state of the patient?
    [1] in severe pain
    [2] in mild or no pain
    Your choice: *why*

I alrready know that
    what the patient is likely to be suffering from
        is rubella /german measles/
so that if
    the state of the patient is in severe pain
then
    the recommendation is see a doctor immediately

    Your choice: *2*

7.2.3 Explanation

The remaining form of explanation, stricly speaking
explaining how, but usually referred to simply as
explanation, occurs usually at the end of the
consultation. The system reaches some conclusion – by
verifying one of its goal hypotheses – and now the user
wants to know just how this conclusion was reached. By
Ennis's definitions, this calls for decribing a process
or a structure: the process of reasoning that was used
or the structure of reasoning leading from the answers
to the conclusion. Again, many systems provide this.
To provide this type of explanation, we need to keep a
record of the answers that the user gave and the rules
that we used to verify the goal hypothesis.

    At least, this is the most general and secure way of
catering for it. However, if we do not make use of
fuzzy or probabilistic rules, we can get away without
any special historical data. The reason for this is
simple: if the explanation generator follows the same
order of processing as the backchainer did, the first
rule that it will find whose antecedents are all

fulfilled and whose conclusion is the item that the explanation was asked for is going to be the same rule as the one that was actually used.

Relying on this, and providing for items that were not given a value or obtained their value from an answer, we can implement a simplified explanation generator. This time, we need to cater for only two things: to receive the request and to process it. We can service this request after the consultation has finished, so we need to alter the top level control slightly (7.4).

```
for each ob in objects                          (7.4)
    set ob.value = 'unknown'
backchain(goals)
print("The results of the consultation are:")
for each ob in objects
    if ob.type = 'goal'
    then print(ob.display, ob.value)
loop
    let cmd = read()
    if cmd = "how" then explain()
until cmd = "end"
```

We must provide some way to end the session; here the user types 'end'. If he types 'how', we let him choose one of the objects (7.5).

```
let explain() =                                 (7.5)
{ print("Which do you want explanation for ?")
  explainone(choose(objects)) }
```

When generating an explanation, we need to take care of three possibilities: the goal was not given a value, the value was received as an answer to a question, and the value was concluded by firing a rule. The outline of the procedure is in (7.6).

```
let explainone(goal) =                          (7.6)
{ if not completed(goal)
  then print_not_established(goal)
  if askable(goal)
  then print_answered_goal(goal)
  else
    { find relevant rule with allvalid antecedents
      print_rule } }
```

We continue with the session shown in section 7.2.2 and exercise the explanation facility. The resulting dialogue is shown here:

The results of the consultation are:

what the patient is likely to be suffering from
        is rubella /german measles/
the recommendation is see a doctor if it gets worse

how

Which do you want explanation for?
   [1] ailment
   [2] recommendation
   [3] temperature
   [4] state
   [5] appearance
   [6] location
   Your choice: *1*

The claim that:

what the patient is likely to be suffering from
    is rubella /german measles/

was established using rule spots3 :

if
    the appearance of the rash is small pink spots
    the temperature of the patient is feverish
then
    what the patient is likely to be suffering from
        is rubella /german measles/

how

Which do you want explanation for?
   [1] ailment
   [2] recommendation
   [3] temperature
   [4] state
   [5] appearance
   [6] location
   Your choice: *2*

The claim that:

the recommendation is see a doctor if it gets worse

was established using rule spots21 :

if
    what the patient is likely to be suffering from
        is rubella /german measles/
    the state of the patient is in mild or no pain
then
    the recommendation is
        see a doctor if it gets worse

how

Which do you want explanation for?
  [1] ailment
  [2] recommendation
  [3] temperature
  [4] state
  [5] appearance
  [6] location
  Your choice: *3*

You said that the temperature of the patient is
feverish

how

Which do you want explanation for?
  [1] ailment
  [2] recommendation
  [3] temperature
  [4] state
  [5] appearance
  [6] location
  Your choice: *6*

A value for the location of the rash was not
established

end

7.3 Uncertainty

One of the strongest claims made in favour of knowledge-based systems is that they can come not only to hard and fast conclusions but also to tentative ones. MYCIN and PROSPECTOR state not only their conclusions but also the degree of confidence that they attach to those conclusions. We shall now examine the mechanisms used to introduce and handle this sort of qualification.

The first point to note is that there is no unique and agreed method of dealing with uncertainties in expert systems. MYCIN and PROSPECTOR use totally different methods. Obviously, the systems spawned from the basis of these two use the method of their parents but, apart from agreement due to inheritance, fundamental differences can be observed between these two families as well as between them and systems cast in different moulds. Just how we should handle uncertainty is the subject of much research and we are a long way from the final answer or even a proposed answer. Indeed, the methods currently in use have come in for a lot of criticism; some authors have gone so far as to say that the methods used cannot be mathematically or logically justified. In spite of this, both systems appear to work satisfactorily, a point of conflict that has yet to be resolved.

Rival schemes have also been proposed and used, but they are very much in need of systematic development and theoretical underpinning. Some systems, most notably R1, use only strict reasoning and do so with great effect. This has led some to advance the claim that, for many applications, the use of non-strict logic is neither necessary nor desirable. It is not necessary because many applications do not require it. Expert systems in the domains of law, company rules, government regulations and the like have no 'fuzziness' about them (not intentionally, anyway). And other applications that could, on the face of it, make good use of probabilities or continuous valued logics – which allow not just 0 and 1 for false and true, but any value in between – do not possess a sufficient descriptive corpus on which to base probabilistic or fuzzy measures. What is the reasonable probability – they ask – of an object on the radar screen being a ship or of a meadow covering a tin mine?

We should take note of their misgivings but decide for ourselves whether these techniques are of use to the problem at hand or not. We can take comfort from the fact that the techniques have been used, and can be used, to good effect should we need them.

7.3.1 PROSPECTOR's scheme

PROSPECTOR marries two different methods of handling uncertainty. The first is based on Bayesian decision theory and relies on the equation from probability theory known as Bayes' rule. The second is a set of formulae for fuzzy logic.

As any elementary textbook on probability theory gives a derivation of Bayes' rule, we shall not derive it here, but concentrate on how PROSPECTOR makes use of it. Let us denote the probability of an event E by $p(E)$ and the probability of a hypothesis H given event E as $p(H|E)$. We can now define two ratios of likelihood:

$$LS = \frac{p(E|H)}{p(E|\text{not } H)} \quad \text{and} \quad LN = \frac{p(\text{not } E|H)}{p(\text{not } E|\text{not } H)}$$

In PROSPECTOR terminology, LS is the *sufficiency measure* and LN the *necessity measure*. A rule describing a plausible relation between an event E and a hypothesis H is written as

if E **then** *(to degree LS, LN)* H

Hypotheses in a model are given *prior* probabilities which, together with the rules and the LS, LN measures are obtained from the expert. To be more precise, because probabilities are computationally awkward to handle, PROSPECTOR uses *odds* rather than probabilities. If we write $o(H)$ for the odds of hypothesis H, we can convert probabilities to odds using the formula

$$o(H) = \frac{p(H)}{1 - p(H)}$$

Whenever we obtain some evidence E, we can calculate the *posterior* probabilities using Bayes' rule. There are three cases to consider:

1. The user states that E is definitely present. We obtain the posterior odds by using the formula

   $o(H|E) = LS * o(H)$

2. The user states that E is definitely not present. We obtain the posterior odds by using the formula

   $o(H|not\ E) = LN * o(H)$

3. The user expresses uncertainty about E on a -5 to +5 scale, where +5 indicates E is definitely present, -5 that it is definitely absent, 0 shows no information, and intermediate values denote degrees of uncertainty. We get the posterior odds by linear interpolation between $o(H|E)$ and $o(H)$ if the answer is positive and between $o(H|not\ E)$ and $o(H)$ if it is negative, scaled by the answer.

Internally, as a further step towards efficiency, PROSPECTOR uses log-odds and addition for these formulae. The formulae, as they stand, have the odds as multiplicative factors. Multiplication, without special hardware, is more expensive than addition. Using the logarithms of odds and of LS and LN, the results can be calculated using the less expensive operation of addition.

The fuzzy set formulae allow conjunctions, disjunctions and negation in the antecedents of rules. The relevant formulae are:

    for conjunction: $p(A\ and\ B) = min(p(A), p(B))$
    for disjunction: $p(A\ or\ B)\ = max(p(A), p(B))$
    for negation: $p(not\ A)\ \ = 1 - p(A)$

The formula for negation is the standard one used in probability theory; it is based on the observation that the probabilities of A and *not* A add up to 1. The formula for the conjunction of two items takes the lesser, and for disjunction the greater of the two values. The intuitive appeal of these formulae is strong: the probability of two events cannot be better than that of the least likely and the probability of either of two events cannot be worse than that of the most likely. It should be pointed out, nevertheless, that these are not the only possible and mathematically justifiable formulations; there are many others.

7.3.2 MYCIN's scheme

When developing MYCIN, Shortliffe recognised that medicine, in many ways a very well quantified discipline, lacks sufficient data and verified models in so many areas that rigorous probabilistic analysis of clinical decision-making is not possible. He developed, therefore, a model of inexact reasoning more suited to diagnostic practice.

MYCIN, like the shell described in chapter 5, records information in attribute-value pairs. Unlike our shell, it can record a number of different values for each attribute differentiated by associated *certainty factors* which express the system's confidence in those values. Rules also carry certainty factors which express the expert's degree of confidence in drawing the conlusion from the antecedents. In essence, a rrule has the form

if *(p1 v1) (p2 v2)*... **then** *(pn vn cf)*

where *cf* is this certainty factor.

When MYCIN activates a rule, it calculates a certainty factor for the antecedents. This is simply the minimum of the certainty factors of the antecedents. Let us call this *af*. Now there are two possibilities: the rule creates a new value or the rule updates an old value.

If the rule creates a new value, it attaches a certainty factor that is the product of the factor calculated for the antecedents and the factor attached to the rule, that is *cf* * *af*. Thus if the minimum factor for the antecedents is 0.6 and the rule's factor is 0.7, the *(pn vn)* will have a certainty factor of 0.42.

If the rule updates an old value, matters are a bit more complicated. The factor *cf* * *af* is still calculated; let us call it *c1*. The factor that is already associated with the attribute/value pair we can call *c2*.

MYCIN uses the following formulae to calculate their combination, which we shall call $c3$:

$$c3 = c2 + c1 - (c2 * c1) \qquad \text{if } c2 > 0 \text{ and } c1 > 0$$
$$c3 = c2 + c1 + (c2 * c1) \qquad \text{if } c2 < 0 \text{ and } c1 < 0$$
$$c3 = 1 \qquad \text{if } c1 = 1 \text{ and } c2 = -1$$
$$\text{or } c2 = 1 \text{ and } c1 = -1$$

$$c3 = \frac{c2 + c1}{1 - min(|c2|,|c1|)} \qquad \text{in all other cases}$$

Shortliffe in *Computer Based Medical Consultation: MYCIN* (1976) gives the derivation for and reasoning behind these formulae. Readers familiar with probability theory will notice their similarity with the formula for the probability of joint events. It is fair to say that - other than in systems based on MYCIN - Shortliffe's method of handling uncertainty has not found wide acceptance; many more systems use PROSPECTOR's scheme.

7.4 Summary

This chapter has given some of the more important extensions to a basic shell. Providing the knowledge engineers and users with these facilities renders the shell usable but not necessarily a convenient and effective tool for implementing expert systems. The knowledge engineer would need other tools to ease his task. A rule editor that allows him to enter, modify, and display rules and their relationships would be one such extension. Another would be a set of tools for performing sensitivity analysis. The user needs some means of volunteering information, of directing the line of investigation, of changing any answer that he has given. And, of course, both need the usual set of commands that provide a path to other system facilities, saving and storing rules, logging sessions, interrupting and resuming consultations, producing and modifying menus and displays, to name but a few.

Further reading

For a very practical treatment of explanations, read Robert H. Ennis's book, *Logic in Teaching* (Prentice-Hall, 1969).

PROSPECTOR's scheme is described in Richard Duda, John Gaschnig and Peter Hart's 'Model Design in the PROSPECTOR Consultant System for Mineral Exploitation' in *Expert Systems in the Micro Electronic Age*, ed. D. Michie (Edinburgh University Press, 1979).

Edward H. Shortliffe describes his reasons for departing from Bayes' rule and the rationale for MYCIN's certainty factor mechanisms in his book, *Computer Based Medical Consultation: MYCIN* (Elsevier, 1976).

8 Practice

Throughout the book we have met applications of expert systems. The question naturally arises: can we make use of the technique and, if so, for what? In this last chapter we shall review the practical guidance that has so far emerged on the application of expert systems to new problems.

Just as Dumas exhorted would-be detectives to *chercher la femme*, would-be users are told to search for the expert. If there is no expert in the field in which we wish to use the system, our chances of success are negligible. If there is an expert - self-confessed or even acknowledged - whose track record is disappointing, we are not likely to do much better with our system. If there is an expert, with a history of good results, but we have no access to him or his know-how, or he is unwilling to cooperate, we will have difficulties in acquiring the rules for our application. In short: no expert means no expert system.

However, not everything that a successful expert does can be captured and reproduced by these techniques. This should come as a comfort and reassurance to experts who feel threatened by these techniques. Expert systems are incapable of innovation and creativity. The knowledge built into them, which is the source of their power, is also the limit of their effectiveness. They can do no more than that which is explicit in or implied by the rules they possess. Even the achievements of apparently creative AI systems like Eurisko, which discovered for example a new VLSI building block, are by the admission of their creator D.B. Lenat '60 per cent Lenat and 40 per cent Eurisko'.

When we talk of 'rules' here, we do not just mean rules of fact. We cannot expect an expert system to reproduce the knowledge and know-how of the electronics industry from Maxwell's equations. It would need also rules of procedure and strategy to do so, and there are no experts for these! So what we can reasonably expect to do is to capture and use what the expert would look upon as mundane and routine in his field. Thus in our search for a likely application we should stay on the side of pragmatic rationalism on the one hand and not try to cross the boundary of creativity on the other.

But even under these restrictions, our choice of what the system could do is still very large. Not merely because with the new tools we can now address new domains, but equally importantly because we can handle those domains differently. The introduction of computers brought not only instrumental but also methodical changes: our approach to describing objectives, tasks and methods had to become more thorough, precise and accurate. Viewed at the programming level, the descriptions had to be complete: having branched on high and equal, we must specify what to do on low. This aspect of computing has led to more headaches, premature decisions, misspecifications and tears than any other. Computer programs are intolerant of gaps. The specification stage of the system life cycle not only lays the foundations for the later stages, it is also an important test of feasibility: if you cannot specify it, you cannot implement it.

The techniques that we have studied in this book make no such demands. An expert system will not collapse for want of rules, or because of gaps or even inconsistencies in those rules. For the first time, we have the means to build a system with incomplete specifications. We can build into it what we know and leave out what we do not without running the risk of crashing it or making it loop forever. Indeed, one could argue that as knowledge knows no bounds, a knowledge based system can never be said to be complete.

This new-found freedom has important consequences not only on tthe applications that we can now choose but also on their implementation and use.

Because the technique is tolerant of gaps, we can take a different approach to implementation. Instead of the customary one-bite-at-the-cherry, straight-line development running from specifications to handover, we can - or even are occasionally forced to - take successive approximations through prototyping. For inexperienced users and organisations - who know neither what is reasonable to attempt nor how much effort it will take - this provides a tremendous advantage. They can tackle a small part of the problem at limited effort and cost, and take frequent decision points on whether to continue with the development and, if so, in what direction.

As these systems are of necessity always incomplete, they will be released for use as such. This has two important implications. One is that the users must be made aware of this fact. To most of them this will represent a radical departure from the rather paternalistic systems that they are used to. While this means that they gain a partner rather than a mechanised taskmaster, it also means that they must again assume responsibility for their actions and examine the system's output with critical eyes.

The second major implication impinges on the tasks of the system's builders. Developing a system through successive prototypes means that what is released to the users is - however well developed - essentially only a prototype. It also means that, because knowledge of · the field and user requirements change and because those changes can now be more easily accommodated, updates to the system will become more frequent. The need for reliable lines of communication to carry feedback from the users becomes essential. And the need for strict version and configuration control becomes more urgent than ever before.

All these are, however, a small price to pay for the extra facility and freedom that they bring.

Epilogue

The time has come to bring this book to a close. These
few chapters have afforded a brief glimpse of the
techniques of expert systems. It is hoped that the
glimpse is sufficient to show that the techniques used
are neither too arcane to comprehend nor too intricate
to implement. In fact their very simplicity can be the
greatest hindrance to assessing their importance and
applicability. Many of Gutenberg's contemporaries must
have wondered what use - never mind what long-term
implications - casting the alphabet in lead could
possibly have. What we have here is equally simple and
equally important. It is easy to appreciate what the
technique offers: an opportunity to solve problems that
we could not tackle before using computers. But to
assess its impact and significance requires the
hindsight of history.

References

Anderson, J., *Language, Memory and Thought*, Erlbaum Associates, 1976.

Barr, A. and Feigenbaum, E., *The Handbook of Artificial Intelligence*, Vols 1-3, Pitman, 1981-3.

Bornat, R.,*Understanding and Writing Compilers*, Macmillan, 1979.

Davis, R. and King, J., 'An overview of production systems' in Elcock, E.W. and Michie, D. (eds), *Machine Intelligence 8*, Ellis Horwood, 1977.

Duda, R., Gaschnig, J. and Hart, P., 'Model Design in the PROSPECTOR Consultant System for Mineral Exploitation' in Michie, D. (ed.), *Expert Systems in the Micro Electronic Age*, Edinburgh University Press, 1979.

Ennis, R.H., *Logic in Teaching*, Prentice-Hall, 1969.

Ernst, G. and Newell, A., *GPS: A Case Study in Generality and Problem Solving*, Academic Press, 1969.

Hayes-Roth, F., Waterman, D.A. and Lenat, D.B., *Building Expert Systems*, Addison-Wesley, 1983.

Henderson, P., *Functional Programming: Application and Implementation*, Prentice-Hall, 1980.

Lindsay, R.K., Buchanan, B.G., Feigenbaum, E.A., and Lederberg, J., *Applications of Artificial Intelligence for Organic Chemistry*, McGraw-Hill, 1980.

McDermott, J., 'XSEL: a computer sales person's assistant', in Hayes, J.E., Michie, D. and Pao, Y-H (eds.), *Machine Intelligence 10*, Ellis Horwood Ltd. and John Wiley & Sons, 1982.

van Melle, William J., *System Aids in Constructing Consultation Programs*, UMI Research Press, 1981.

Minsky, M., *Computation: Finite and Infinite Machines*, Prentice-Hall, 1967.

References

Newell, A. and Simon, H., *Human Problem Solving*,
Prentice-Hall, 1972.

Nilsson, N., *Principles of Artificial
Intelligence*, Springer-Verlag, 1982.

Post, E., 'Formal reductions of the general
combinatorial decision problem' in *American Journal
of Mathematics, Vol. 65*, 1943.

Shortliffe, E.H., *Computer Based Medical
Consultation: MYCIN*, Elsevier, 1976.

Sowa, J.F., *Conceptual Structures: Information
Processing in Mind and Machine*, Addison-Wesley,
1984.

Turing, A.M., 'Can a Machine Think?' in Feigenbaum,
E.A. and Feldman, J. (eds), *Computers and
Thought*, McGraw-Hill, 1963.

Vickers, Sir Geoffrey, *The Art of Judgement: A
Study in Policy Making*, University Paperbacks,
Methuen, 1968.

Winston, P.H. and Horn, B.K.P., *LISP*,
Addison-Wesley, 1981.

Index